The Year Rock Became Mainstream

John Van der Kiste

sonicbondpublishing.com

Sonicbond Publishing Limited
www.sonicbondpublishing.co.uk
Email: info@sonicbondpublishing.co.uk

First Published in the United Kingdom 2021
First Published in the United States 2021

British Library Cataloguing in Publication Data:
A Catalogue record for this book is available from the British Library

Copyright John Van der Kiste 2021

ISBN 978-1-78952-147-4

Typeset in ITC Garamond & ITC Avant Garde
Printed and bound in England

Graphic design and typesetting: Full Moon Media

1970

a year in
Rock

The Year Rock Became Mainstream

John Van der Kiste

sonicbondpublishing.com

1970

a year in rock
The Year Rock Became Mainstream

Contents

Foreword and Acknowledgements

In 1970 I was a teenager at school, studying for O-levels, either to the accompaniment of Radio 1 (long before the days of stereo FM broadcasting) or a small collection of long-playing vinyl albums, whether my own or borrowed from friends. Didn't we all? Yet there was undeniably something *different* about 1970. It was the year that everyone's favourite group, The Beatles, startled us by owning up and publicly admitting they could no longer work together; we suddenly lost Jimi Hendrix; buying pop singles became passé, and being seen with the latest Zeppelin or Pink Floyd album or current issue of *Melody Maker* was much cooler than having a Jackson Five or Tremeloes single in your hand. And you were also forever checking the music press full-page adverts from new mail-order company, Virgin Records, that sold LPs postage free at five shillings (25 pence) cheaper than your local record shop.

More than half a century later, much of the best music of that year still evokes the sheer magic of that time. For me, it will never fade. I hope this book conveys to others some of the unique musical flavour of those momentous twelve months.

Particular thanks are due to Stephen Lambe and everyone else at Sonicbond for their encouragement with and help in this project; to Ray Dorset, Francis Jansen, Kev Hunter, Alan Taylor and Derek Wadeson, for information and supplying illustrations; and as ever to my long-suffering wife Kim, for her constant support.

Chart positions are from the Official Music Charts Company (UK) and Billboard (US), which vary slightly from those published each week in *Melody Maker* and *NME (New Musical Express)*.

```
1   (1)  TWO LITTLE BOYS ......................... Rolf Harris, Columbia
2   (2)  MELTING POT ................................... Blue Mink, Philips
3   (5)  TRACY ................................................ Cuff Links, MCA
4   (4)  ALL I HAVE TO DO IS DREAM
                        Bobbie Gentry and Glen Campbell, Capitol
5   (3)  RUBY DON'T TAKE YOUR LOVE TO TOWN
                        Kenny Rogers and the 1st Edition, Reprise
6   (6)  SUSPICIOUS MINDS ......................... Elvis Presley, RCA
7   (7)  SUGAR, SUGAR ................................... Archies, RCA
8  (10)  PLAY GOOD OLD ROCK 'N' ROLL ... Dave Clark Five, Columbia
9  (24)  REFLECTIONS OF MY LIFE .................... Marmalade, Decca
10   (8)  YESTER-ME, YESTER-YOU, YESTERDAY
                        Stevie Wonder, Tamla Motown
11   (9)  ONION SONG ... Marvin Gaye and Tammi Terrell, Tamla Motown
12  (12)  WITHOUT LOVE ................................ Tom Jones, Decca
13  (15)  LEAVIN' DURHAM TOWN ........... Roger Whittaker, Columbia
14  (13)  LIQUIDATOR .................... Harry J and the All Stars, Trojan
15  (10)  WINTER WORLD OF LOVE ..... Engelbert Humperdinck, Decca
16  (17)  SOMEDAY WE'LL BE TOGETHER
                        Diana Ross and the Supremes, Tamla Motown
17   (—)  FRIENDS ............................................. Arrival, Decca
18  (22)  COMIN' HOME ...... Delaney and Bonnie and Friends, Atlantic
19  (14)  (CALL ME) NUMBER ONE ..................... Tremeloes, CBS
20   (—)  COME AND GET IT ............................... Badfinger, Apple
21  (18)  GREEN RIVER ........... Creedence Clearwater Revival, Liberty
22  (20)  HIGHWAY SONG ........................... Nancy Sinatra, Reprise
23  (23)  BUT YOU LOVE ME DADDY ....... ........ Jim Reeves, RCA
24  (16)  LOVE IS ALL ..................... Malcolm Roberts, Major Minor
25  (29)  WITH THE EYES OF A CHILD .......... Cliff Richard, Columbia
26   (—)  IF I THOUGHT YOU'D CHANGE YOUR MIND
                        Cilla Black, Parlophone
27  (19)  SOMETHING ...................................... Beatles, Apple
28   (—)  SEVENTH SON ......................... Georgie Fame, CBS
29  (21)  LONELINESS .......................... Des O'Connor, Columbia
30   (—)  SHE SOLD ME MAGIC ..................... Lou Christie, Buddah
```

pop 30 publishers

1 Herman Darewski; 2 Cookaway; 3 Maurice; 4   Carlin; 17 Carlin/Equity; 18 Famous Chappell; 19
Acuff-Rose; 5 Southern; 6 London Tree; 7 Wel-   Gale; 20 Northern Songs; 21 Jondora; 22 April;

Above: A January chart from Melody Maker. Middle-of-the-road entertainers, plus
The Beatles and Elvis Presley, still hold their own against competition from Motown,
bubblegum pop and reggae.

Introduction

Only a few weeks into 1970, it became apparent that popular music in Britain and America was undergoing a massive change. During the late 1960s, there had been something of a divide between pop and rock music that gradually narrowed as the decade finished. By summer, the line between both was becoming even less marked, with more common ground between what constituted the singles and albums charts. Singles from groups once labelled as underground, progressive or heavy rock were moving further into the mainstream, and appearing on daytime radio and television with a regularity that would have been almost unthinkable a year earlier. Pop was catchy and commercial, for teenagers, radio and the Top 30, 'but its detractors saw it as trivial and insubstantial. Rock, on the other hand, was meant to be authentic and artistic ... worthy but difficult' [Sandbrook, p.559]. Economics played a part as well, for rock-loving adults could afford to spend more on albums than the younger 45s-loving generation. Moreover, 'rock was not only a thousand watts louder, it was also a thousand times more serious'. [Norman, p.284]

Now they were becoming as one. Several groups who had largely been known for three-minute pop singles began to produce more adventurous or sophisticated work, partly to appeal to an older and more discerning audience, partly to break out of the straitjacket of recording songs from a music publisher at the behest of a hits-hungry record company holding a metaphorical gun at their heads to sell singles to a teenage fan base who would soon mature and leave yesterday's pin-up idols behind. Some of them found it necessary to disband and reform, often with a change in personnel and maybe under a new name. Others who had formed late in the previous decade to follow a direction beyond the three-minute song in favour of hard rock, blues, jazz, folk or classical influences, to say nothing of extended jamming sessions and the odd track that took up one entire side of an album, often had a foot in at least two camps. The old underground was now rock, be it jazz-rock, folk-rock, prog-rock, blues-rock, even pop-rock, or maybe an amalgam of everything. Old boundaries were being broken down. Did the old pigeonholes still matter?

Rock festivals became more frequent, helping to establish or confirm the reputations of certain artists, who would be rewarded with substantially increased album sales. The music on those albums developed in terms of complexity, as did the packaging. Gatefold sleeves had once been the preserve of a few major names; now almost every act considered them essential. In 1969 record companies had been preparing themselves for the new decade by launching or developing their own 'progressive' labels. EMI Records introduced Harvest, to be followed by Philips' Vertigo, and Pye's Dawn. They helped to introduce their signings to a wider audience, largely less affluent students, with various artists samplers, usually double albums, at a budget price, like Harvest's *Picnic: A Breath of Fresh Air* and Vertigo's *Vertigo Annual*. One of the most successful was CBS's *Fill Your Head With Rock*, which balanced a selection of British and American acts across its four sides.

Its compiler David Howell stated that its release was part of a major push to establish CBS as 'the top label in contemporary music', aware that acts like Chicago, Santana, Al Stewart, Leonard Cohen, Argent, Skin Alley, and Taj Mahal were not necessarily less important than ever-dependable middle-of-the-road stars such as Andy Williams and Barbra Streisand.

Moreover, an album no longer had to be the end product of several weeks' or months' painstaking work in the studio. Live recordings appeared partly as a quicker way of fulfilling contractual obligations should a group or artist be keen to move on and negotiate a more lucrative deal elsewhere, and partly to beat the bootleggers at their own game. The previous year had seen the burgeoning of bootleg albums, often very expensive, breaking every law of copyright, clandestinely manufactured and distributed without the artists ever receiving a penny in royalties. As they could only be purchased on the sly from selective retailers (and not the squeaky-clean high street chains), they were highly desirable, and collections of previously unreleased studio recordings by Bob Dylan that found their way onto vinyl were soon followed by live sets from many a major act. Releasing officially approved in concert LPs were a more effective way of combating the trade than trying to track down every retail outlet or fly-by-night pressing plant responsible in order to seize and destroy their stock.

No less importantly, 1970 was the year that the group who had completely dominated the music scene of the 1960s disbanded, and the year that the man revered as the most innovative and flamboyant guitarist of all time suddenly died.

The swinging sixties were over. They had brought their own musical revolution and had shown a glimpse of what innovations might be possible in building on and adapting old traditions and bringing new ideas to the table. There had been dark moments along the way, and it was ironic that a decade that had often been swept along in a mood of optimism should have been brought almost to a juddering halt in December 1969 by the Altamont Festival, in which four people lost their lives. January 1970 would herald a new dawn.

Overview

Changes

For the first few weeks of 1970, it seemed as if nothing had really changed. As the new year and decade started, the British album chart was topped by The Beatles' *Abbey Road,* followed by Tom Jones's *Live in Las Vegas* and the compilation *Motown Chartbusters Volume 3.* Rolf Harris had the No. 1 single with 'Two Little Boys', followed by hits from Kenny Rogers and the First Edition, the bleak anti-war country ballad 'Ruby Don't Take Your Love to Town', and from Blue Mink, a plea for racial integration and harmony, 'Melting Pot', respectively.

That same week Bob Harris, a young journalist with a passion for music, was invited to write an article for *Friends,* the British equivalent of *Rolling Stone* magazine, on Radio 1. A few weeks later, he was recording a pilot show for the station and soon after that, he was a regular presenter himself. Years later, he wrote in his memoirs that he was out of work, his wife Sue was at college, and they had very little money. Yet as they listened to church bells ringing in the new year, there was a tremendous sense of excitement: 'I had the strongest possible feeling that 1970 was going to be a good year.' [Harris, p.35] It would be a very good year indeed for music.

Meanwhile, John Peel was featuring sessions by Roy Harper, Family and Tyrannosaurus Rex on his BBC Radio 1 evening programme. Peel was always the least conformist of the station's presenters, with his shoulder-length hair and readiness to cock a snook at the establishment now and again, sail close to the wind on occasion, and get away with nothing more than a metaphorical smack on the wrist. He and his producer, John Walters, were strongly committed to championing the music of the unknown [Garner, p.67]. During the year, they would record and broadcast sessions from an eclectic roster, including Bridget St John, Van der Graaf Generator, Third Ear Band, Michael Chapman, Dr Strangely Strange, and The Incredible String Band, who would remain cult names that never scaled the heights. Others would go on to achieve success, notably Argent, Renaissance, Supertramp, Hawkwind, Ralph McTell, and Curved Air, who were well ahead of their time in issuing their debut album, *Air Conditioning,* later that year. It was available not only in black vinyl but also as a limited edition picture disc, though the technology was still in its infancy and the latter's sound quality compared poorly with conventional vinyl. Another important name on the list was Medicine Head, who would later give Peel's Dandelion label its only taste of chart success during three years of fitful life. Dandelion was Peel's way of getting unreleased music he particularly enjoyed onto record without necessarily expecting commercial success, and in fact, he reckoned that every such release lost him money. One of its most eccentric 45s that year was 'On Ilkla Moor Baht 'at', by comedian Bill Oddie, the old Yorkshire folk song rearranged as a parody of Joe Cocker's 'With a Little Help From My Friends'. The session players included two members of Cocker's Grease Band, who had played with him at the Woodstock festival, plus Mott the

Hoople organist Verden Allen, and Traffic drummer Jim Capaldi.

Tin Pan Alley pop still ruled part of the time, with bespoke songwriters and producers calling the tune in more ways than one. The first new No. 1 of the year was 'Love Grows (Where My Rosemary Goes)', a naggingly catchy bubblegum number written by Tony Macaulay and Barry Mason, and recorded by Edison Lighthouse, a studio group assembled largely for the purpose. The vocalist was Tony Burrows, an experienced session singer who had the unusual distinction of handling lead vocals on two other records that were simultaneously hits for other acts, White Plains and Brotherhood of Man – and who inevitably became a regular on BBC TV's weekly chart show, *Top of the Pops*, fronting two of the three groups in the studio in the same programme with a quick costume change. Dubbed by some 'the most successful unknown singer in Britain', he would later claim to have appeared on about a hundred Top 20 hits in the 1970s. Hardly anybody over the age of fourteen would ever own up to liking 'Love Grows', but it still topped the charts for five weeks, and also reached the American top five. Burrows was one of many who benefited from the industry of tried and tested songwriting teams like Roger Cook and Roger Greenaway, Guy Fletcher and Doug Flett, Mitch Murray and Peter Callender, supplying hits for groups and singers, including specially created studio acts as well as established performers like The Hollies and Cliff Richard, who often relied on music publishers to find their next potential chart 45.

Some were more content with the situation than others. Among those who chafed at the system were The Sweet, who played hard rock on stage but at first reluctantly bowed to pressure by recording more commercial fare on two singles released that year, the Cook-Greenaway composition 'All You'll Ever Get From Me', and a song originally written for American cartoon group The Archies, 'Get on the Line'. Their newest member, guitarist Andy Scott, spoke for many of his peers in admitting that he was selling his soul to the devil by joining a pop group. 'Having been in this progressive band that was 'Here for the vibe, man!', I wanted to pay the rent as well.' [Thompson, p.54] By contrast, singer Johnny Johnson was happy to go with the flow. He had fronted a vocal group, The Bandwagon, who formed in America three years earlier but found their brand of Northern soul much more popular in Britain and Europe. After they disbanded, he retained the name, recording, appearing on TV and touring with various backing vocalists as Johnny Johnson and His Bandwagon, based in Britain. Two more top ten hits resulted in 1970, the most successful being a Macaulay-Cook-Greenaway number, '(Blame It) on the Pony Express'.

Although it still honoured its basic function of reflecting the current Top 30 and appealing to parents as well as kids, *Top of the Pops* realised it must move with the changing times. By the end of January, it had expanded from 30 to 45 minutes and made an effort to feature more left-field acts alongside chart fare. The first regular full-length show, on 29 January, included an eclectic line-up of hits and new releases, presented by the infamous Jimmy Savile. As well as mainstream pop by Edison Lighthouse, Mary Hopkin, Jonathan King and Brotherhood of Man (a different line-up from the quartet who would win the Eurovision Song Contest in 1976), it also included more rock-oriented hits by Chicago, Jethro Tull, Badfinger and Canned Heat – some of the latter seen bopping around to their hit 'Let's Work Together' with the predominantly teenage studio audience, and then presenting prizes of the week's Top 10 singles to one male and one female who had been adjudged the best dancers. Most innovative of all, the two new releases represented what was considered the 'new music', 'Sympathy' by Rare Bird, which would later reach the Top 30, and opening the show, 'Same Old Story' by Blodwyn Pig, a group formed by ex-Jethro Tull guitarist Mick Abrahams, who were little heard of again. The programme featured an equally diverse bill of fare during the next few months, including King Crimson, Country Joe, Caravan, and the then still little-known skinhead band Slade, whose radical change of image a year later would help make them one of the most successful British acts of the decade.

In the era of three-channel television programming (BBC1, BBC2 and ITV), there was little alternative. Popular music documentaries were very rare, and the only other regular choice in 1970, apart from a short season of *In Concert* on BBC between October and December, was *Disco 2*, also BBC2. A 25-minute magazine format weekly programme that went out late at night presented first by Tommy Vance and then by Pete Drummond, both from Radio 1, it featured largely album-orientated rock, blues and folk acts, both live in the studio and on film. After three separate series, it was superseded in 1971 by the long-running *The Old Grey Whistle Test*.

Two particularly noteworthy performers on *TOTP* in February were John Lennon and Yoko Ono, the former making his first appearance on the programme for nearly four years. Though he had been asked not to go public for business reasons, the previous September, Lennon had told an increasingly weary Paul McCartney that he 'wanted a divorce' and was leaving The Beatles. Thrilled by the freedom of being his own boss at last, he, Ono and the Plastic Ono Band, a name applied to whichever collective of friends and musicians who were available when required, had just made their first single of the decade. 'Instant Karma!' was written, recorded and produced by Phil Spector in a day and released ten days later. Eager to promote it as widely as possible, they recorded four performances in the TV studio, two of which were selected for broadcast, and were duly rewarded with a transatlantic smash, reaching five in the UK and seven in the USA.

The end of the old order: The Beatles; Simon and Garfunkel

Since the days of Beatlemania in 1963, the Beatles had dominated popular music on both sides of the Atlantic and through much of the world, and it seemed almost unthinkable that life could go on without a new single or album from the Fab Four at least two or three times a year. But by 1969, it was clear that with increasing personal, musical and business differences that were no longer possible to shield from an ever-inquisitive press, their days as a unit were numbered.

The last few painful weeks from January 1970 onwards almost resembled a real-life soap opera. Lennon and Ono had already released two experimental avant-garde albums (in his words, 'avant-garde' was French for bullshit – well, he said it), as had George Harrison, while in March Ringo Starr unveiled his first solo project, *Sentimental Journey*, comprising twelve standards mostly from the pre-rock'n'roll era, with orchestral arrangements. Paul McCartney had also prepared an album, *McCartney*, recorded mostly at home, featuring him on all instruments and vocals, apart from his wife Linda's harmonies. He had become increasingly estranged from Lennon, Starr and Harrison, after the appointment of Allen Klein as their manager the previous year. His choice had been George Eastman, his father-in-law, and he distrusted Klein, an opinion the others would soon come to share.

The last straw for the already divided group, now effectively if secretly a trio post-Lennon, came when McCartney was asked by the other three to delay release of his solo album so it would not clash with the appearance of their ready-to-go *Let It Be*. He was determined to schedule his album for April 17 release, and the others reluctantly conceded. When he phoned Lennon to say that 'I'm doing what you did', by issuing his own album and leaving the group as well, Lennon answered, 'Good. That makes two of us who have seen sense.' The news made headlines throughout the world. If Lennon, Harrison and Starr were annoyed at first, they later admitted that McCartney's forcing the issue had come as a huge relief. The latter denied that he had left The Beatles, saying that The Beatles had left The Beatles. Lennon quipped, 'Paul hasn't left. I've sacked him.'

'Let It Be' had been released as a single early in March and entered the charts at number two in the UK, going one place higher in America, but suffering the indignity of being held from the top at home by gravel-voiced actor Lee Marvin's 'Wand'rin' Star', from the soundtrack LP of the musical *Paint Your Wagon*. Although the Beatles' album, previously known as *Get Back*, had been ostensibly completed the previous year, produced by George Martin, as usual, the group were dissatisfied with it. Glyn Johns, the engineer, had prepared an acetate of several songs, one copy of which arrived in America and was played by several radio stations, but they could not agree on a running order, or indeed whether to release it at all. Thrilled with his work on 'Instant Karma!', Lennon passed the tapes to Spector and asked him to finish the work they had all evaded for several months. The American producer accordingly removed one track, substituted another, added some studio banter and choral and orchestral overdubs to four tracks. Lennon praised the result, saying Spector had done a great job with 'the shittiest load of badly recorded shit'. [Wenner] Harrison and Starr were satisfied, but McCartney was furious at the alterations to one of his songs, 'The Long and Winding Road'. He demanded specific changes to Spector's treatment of the song in writing, but his letter was received too late.

With Spector credited as producer instead of Martin, the album reached the shops on 8 May and entered the charts in the UK and number one, staying there for three weeks. Although greeted with enthusiasm by fans, this final album of fresh material compared poorly with their previous album *Abbey Road,* the last one they recorded, although it had been released in September 1969. Although not a single in Britain, leaving the way open to Ray Morgan's cover version, 'The Long and Winding Road' would give them a final US number one that summer.

Once the old Beatles were no more, some of the media promptly began a search for someone to fill the vacuum. The group who came closest were Badfinger, another four-piece on the Apple label. Similarities and connections were numerous. In guitarist Pete Ham and bassist Tom Evans they had two joint lead vocalists and a strong songwriting partnership, their album *No Dice* including a track 'Without You' that would be covered by Nilsson (a number one on both sides of the Atlantic) in 1972, and almost equally successful for Mariah Carey in 1994. Moreover, their first hit as Badfinger in 1970, the single 'Come and Get It', had been written and produced by McCartney. Two more top ten singles would follow in the next couple of years, and they were the only group signed to Apple other than The Beatles to have any top ten singles in Britain.

Otherwise, Apple's greatest hope remained Mary Hopkin, who would continue her chart run during the year with three more hits, notably the British Eurovision Song Contest entry 'Knock Knock, Who's There' a song she found thoroughly embarrassing. Out of the 100 songs submitted as possibles for her to sing in the contest, she said she only liked two – and the one chosen was one she loathed. As it did so well in the charts, it meant that she had to include it in her summer season shows that year. 'Standing on a stage singing a song you hate is awful,' she admitted nearly forty years later, by which time she was long retired from live performances. 'Unless you're expressing what's inside there's just no point.' [Robinson] Like several previous British entries, it was placed second in the contest, narrowly beaten in the contest by Ireland's Dana with 'All Kinds of Everything', number one in the UK for two weeks that spring.

The album that had kept *McCartney* from the summit and would reclaim pole position from *Let It Be* was another farewell effort, the last fruits of the often-sparring Paul Simon and Art Garfunkel partnership. When they asked Clive Davis, head of Columbia Records, to choose a first single from *Bridge Over Troubled Water*, they expected it to be the more commercial 'Cecilia', but he told them it had to be the haunting, gospel-sounding title track. They argued that a ballad lasting almost five minutes would have no chance of being played on the radio (Had they forgotten The Beatles' seven-minute 'Hey Jude'?). Davis insisted, and the result made number one on both sides of the Atlantic that spring. Simon had been astonished when he heard 'Let It Be', remarking on the similarities between them with their messages of hope and peace. Another coincidence was that both writers had considered offering them to Aretha Franklin. McCartney had submitted a demo of 'Let It Be' to her producer Jerry Wexler, and her version appeared on the album *This Girl's in Love With You* in January. She did not want it released as a single, which was fortuitous as McCartney sent Wexler a 'legal notice' to prevent them from doing so. In March 1971, 'Bridge' was a single for her, reaching number six but a failure in Britain.

Bridge Over Troubled Water also entered the album chart at number one, holding the peak position in America for ten weeks and Britain for 33 non-consecutive weeks in the next eighteen months, a feat still unsurpassed by any other non-soundtrack album, and the best-selling LP in Britain of the 1970s. Simon and Garfunkel played five European shows in April and May, two in America in July, and then went their separate ways.

The Rolling Stones; The Who; live albums and festivals

Since 1963, a friendly rivalry had existed between The Beatles and The Rolling Stones, even to the point of ensuring that neither group released a new single in the same week to ensure both of them had a fair chance of reaching number one. By 1968, the Stones' productivity had dwindled to only one new 45 and one LP per year. Once the Liverpudlian quartet had ceased to exist, the competition was no longer there, and the sole product coming from the Dartford quintet was *Get Yer Ya-Ya's Out!*, a live souvenir of two American concerts the previous November. Otherwise, barring a solo Mick Jagger single, 'Memo From Turner', from the soundtrack of his 1968 film *Performance*, and now a modest hit (32 in the UK), their main activity that year was to complete another studio album and negotiate a new contract that would include the launch of their own record label. One song they had recorded late in 1969, 'Brown Sugar', received its first live (if private) performance at Keith Richards's 27th birthday party in December 1970, with Eric Clapton guesting on guitar. It was considered for release as a single the next year, but in the end, the early, rather more polished version would be the one made available. The 'party' performance, including Clapton, would not be officially released for over forty years.

Arguably the third most important and consistently successful British group of the 1960s was The Who. In his memoirs, Pete Townshend looked back on this period when the Stones had been through the 'awful, stigmatising tragedy' of deaths in the audience at the Altamont Festival in December 1969, and The Beatles split only a few weeks later. 'In contrast, The Who seemed to have the gods on our side.' They beat the Stones in the live album stakes by recording their own set, *Live at Leeds* at the city university in February, and releasing it three months later.

Another of the year's most successful live albums was *Mad Dogs and Englishmen* by Joe Cocker. Despite two Top 10 singles at the end of the 1960s, the first a chart-topping reworking of The Beatles' 'With a Little Help From My Friends', the Sheffield-born soul singer found more success in America, and in

March 1970, he was told that his management had organised a stateside tour comprising 48 shows in 52 days, due to start in eight days' time. A band of mainly American musicians and backing vocalists was quickly recruited by Leon Russell, who had written his second hit, 'Delta Lady', and his producer Denny Cordell. Although an exhausting experience for the singer, it yielded a double album released that summer, and his first to make the British chart (reaching number 16 and number two in the US). One reviewer praised some tracks while noting that the ensemble was 'formed on a few days' notice to meet contractual obligations, and sounds like, well, like a group that was 'formed on a few days' notice to meet contractual obligations'.

If the live album began to come into its own in 1970, so did the rock festival. In January 1970, John Lennon and Yoko Ono were party to a plan to take part in a music and peace conference near Toronto in July, a follow up on a larger scale to the hastily organised Rock & Roll Revival in which a hurriedly put-together Plastic Ono Band had played the previous autumn. Largely due to Lennon's insistence that admission should be free and fears that it could bring another Altamont-like tragedy in its wake, it was abandoned.

Several smaller-scale events were staged that year, most of those in England benefiting from an unusually hot dry summer, with some more memorable than others. That they often made a massive financial loss, due in part largely to the determination of punters who would storm the barriers without paying in the conviction that such events must be free to all, much to the disgust of those who had paid for their tickets, should not be overlooked. In June, The Bath Festival of Blues and Progressive Music, to give its full title, hosted a bill including Led Zeppelin, Pink Floyd, The Moody Blues, Fairport Convention, Canned Heat and Steppenwolf. Two months later, the Isle of Wight was headlined by Jimi Hendrix in what would be his last English show, plus The Who, Free, Jethro Tull, Family, Taste, Joni Mitchell and Leonard Cohen. Hendrix died suddenly less than a month later, deeply mourned by the music world, making 'Voodoo Chile', a two-year-old album track by The Jimi Hendrix Experience, the year's most unlikely chart-topping single.

One of the most talked-about events was the Hollywood Festival at Newcastle-under-Lyme in May. The audience saw Black Sabbath, Traffic, Colosseum, Free and, making their first British appearance, Grateful Dead – but the previously unknown Mungo Jerry stole the show. Coming onstage after Grateful Dead's lengthy laid-back set that had most of the stoned or drunk audience half-asleep, they fired everyone up with a riotous feelgood set of skiffle and jug band blues that went down so well on the Saturday that they were called back to play again the following night.

Ironically, one song they omitted was their newly-released single 'In the Summertime', leaving the disc jockey to spin it afterwards. For the next few days, the song was barely off the radio, and it became the biggest hit of the summer (number one in the UK for seven weeks, and a number three in the US), as well as topping the charts in several other countries across the world.

The British release set a new trend in being a maxi-single in a picture sleeve, playing at 33 r.p.m. and with twice as much music (three or four tracks per side) as a conventional two-track 45 disc, although smaller numbers of 45s were pressed for jukeboxes. The song aptly summed up a happy-go-lucky, carefree spirit of seasonal joys, becoming the most successful summer hit of all time in terms of airplay and global sales. It was subsequently criticised for its lack of political correctness with its mildly sexist lyrics, although that was hardly new in popular song. Moreover, the line 'have a drink, have a drive', which the group's front man and main songwriter Ray Dorset admitted with hindsight was unwise, would later be used in a government campaign warning against such an offence.

New year, new artistic freedom

For some groups, the dawning of a new year meant a new sense of artistic freedom. The Beatles had ended their days almost like four solo performers acting as session players on each others' songs, while others also welcomed the chance to regroup, diversify or even change style completely. By the beginning of 1970, Love Affair had joined the ranks of those who wearied of being a hit machine, with vocalist Steve Ellis singing on A-sides of singles while the playing was left to session musicians, arrangers and producers. At the start of the new year, he left for a solo career, while the others recruited a new front man, Auguste Eadon, to record more experimental self-penned fare. Neither party ever troubled the charts again, not for want of trying or lack of critical acclaim, for Ellis had always been rightly respected by his peers as a powerful singer. Amen Corner semi-disbanded, with vocalist Andy Fairweather-Low, keyboard player Blue Weaver and drummer Dennis Bryon promptly forming a new outfit, Fair Weather, and had one further burst of success that summer with 'Natural Sinner' (reaching number six in the UK).

The main group to emerge from the blues boom of two years earlier, Fleetwood Mac, had rivalled The Beatles in terms of British record sales success in 1969. Their lucky streak came to an end in the spring when frontman Peter Green left, his mental health issues exacerbated by a bad acid trip on a European tour. Just before his departure he took part in their final recording session together, which produced a single, 'The Green Manalishi (With the Two-Pronged Crown)'. An eerie, unsettling piece featuring some of his most haunting guitar work ever, he claimed that the song was about money, as represented by the devil. Although successful at home, (reaching number ten) it would be the start of a difficult, hitless period for the group with regular line-up changes as they gradually left the blues behind, becoming a hugely popular Anglo-American soft rock ensemble.

Some of their contemporaries also had mixed fortunes. The Tremeloes had also tired of churning out party-style hits, generally written by others, in favour of their own material. It almost proved a foolhardy gesture when their first single of 1970 was the more ambitious, mellotron-driven acoustic ballad and minor hit 'By the Way', a last-minute change of schedule after they had recorded and almost released 'Yellow River', written by guitarist Jeff Christie. The latter promptly formed his own group, Christie, issued an almost identical version and within weeks found themselves at the pinnacle that summer (number one in the UK, 23 in the US). Persevering, The Tremeloes landed themselves another hit that autumn with 'Me and My Life', a UK number four. Full of confidence, they launched a self-penned album *Master* with a car crash of a *Melody Maker* interview in which they – or rather their leader, Alan Blakley – announced they were 'going heavy' and dismissed their earlier records as 'music for morons'. *Master* was a good solid album that demonstrated their songwriting abilities and instrumental skills, but the critics tore them apart, and despite several more singles that were well up to standard, their chart career stalled after one more Top 40 hit the following year.

More lasting success awaited Marmalade. They had formed about four years earlier, achieving a measure of critical acclaim as well as admiration from their peers, notably Jimi Hendrix, for a couple of psych-pop singles, written by vocalist Dean Ford (real name Thomas McAleese) and Wullie (Junior) Campbell that never charted in Britain, and yielded to pressure to record tailor-made hits by other writers. In 1969 they signed a new contract with Decca Records, guaranteeing them the final say in what they recorded. The first result of their born-again phase was the introspective 'Reflections of My Life'. When they played it to a senior company executive, he liked it but suggested it would stand a better chance without the unusual reverse guitar solo. Did he know, they asked, why they had signed to a new label? 'The £105,000 advance,' he replied. They shook their heads. They said at the time, 'It was total artistic control, and no record company interference!' Having won their battle, they were rewarded with a transatlantic hit (a UK number three and a US number ten). A subsequent 45, the folksy 'Rainbow', enjoyed similar success that summer (again, number three in the UK but number 51 in the USA), and the American success of their album *Reflections of the Marmalade* (reaching number 71) proved it was no flash in the pan.

One group that proved that a complete overhaul, not merely in musical but also sartorial terms, could be beneficial were Status Quo. Trading in their colourful jackets and frilly shirts for ripped scruffy jeans and dirty trainers, and determined not to be 'a pretty little pop band', they set out their stall in March with the driving boogie of 'Down the Dustpipe'. 'Down the drainpipe for this one!' quipped Radio 1 presenter Tony Blackburn disdainfully after playing it on his breakfast show. Nevertheless, a punishing schedule of live gigs in back rooms of pubs and similar small venues instead of the Mecca ballrooms circuit, at which they refused to play their earlier hits – and despite jibes that they were three-chord merchants, 'the poor man's Canned Heat', or just another band gone heavy to fit the times – they eventually found a faithful new audience. As Francis Rossi put it, they were ready for a change of direction and image. 'We weren't an overnight success; there were times when we first started in the underground clubs where people sat listening as if they couldn't be bothered, stoned out of their minds.' Rick Parfitt added that the change gradually paid off: Rossi and Parfitt said in the band's autobiography: 'But we went on and strutted our stuff because we were confident. We were pretty heavily armed with some good material and we liked what we were doing.' 'Dustpipe' slowly but surely penetrated the airwaves (number 12 in the UK), and a second single that year, the lazy rolling blues 'In My Chair' (number 21 in the UK), launched an almost unbroken string of hits into the 21st century, and their album *Ma Kelly's Greasy Spoon* laid the groundwork as well.

Occasionally, for a group to lose their driving force could be only a temporary setback. The Small Faces had been left rudderless in 1969 when their frustrated front man Steve Marriott walked out on them to form Humble Pie. Within months, they had acquired two ex-members of The Jeff Beck Group, vocalist Rod Stewart and guitarist Ron Wood. After Wood and Small Faces keyboard player Ian McLagan had played on Stewart's first solo album, *An Old Raincoat Won't Ever Let You Down* a regrouping became evident. Shortening their name, as the two new members were both almost six foot tall, The Faces were soon in business with their debut album, *First Step* though for contractual reasons, the American issue was still credited to The Small Faces. Stewart still pursued his solo career, releasing a second album, *Gasoline Alley* (62 in the UK, but 27 in the USA) that summer. One of their most fervent champions was John Peel, who once called them his all-time favourite live band. There may have been better groups, he said, 'but there was never a band to make you feel so good'. A lasting bond was formed backstage at a gig in Newcastle City Hall when they burst in on him and invited him for a drink. Not being an imbiber at the time, he watched them disappearing into their dressing room for a party characterised by scantily clad women, breaking glass and curries being flung against walls. What dreadful rowdy people, he thought at first, before realising that they were having a far better time than he was. As for the music, it 'exactly defined the band', with no pretence whatsoever, recapturing for him the kind of feelings he had when he first heard people like Little Richard and Jerry Lee Lewis.

Another group that began the decade with a significant change of personnel likewise sowing the seeds of a long career were The Move. Having opened their assault on the charts with a couple of hits that took elements from psychedelia, hard rock and American West Coast-like vocal harmonies, they parted company with their vocalist Carl Wayne and recruited Jeff Lynne, formerly frontman of the critically respected but still hitless Idle Race. Lynne and Roy Wood, their guitarist, principal songwriter and now undisputed front man, not only planned to take The Move in a different musical direction, but also to launch the Electric Light Orchestra, a group including classically-trained string players, and with a repertoire that fused rock and classical styles. To finance such an undertaking required The Move to continue selling records, and their first single of 1970, the growling guitar riff-driven 'Brontosaurus' (a number seven UK hit), came as a surprise after their previous easy-on-the-ear releases. They released two very eclectic albums in 1970, *Shazam*, featuring Wayne but issued just after his departure, and *Looking On*, which was largely the brainchild of Wood and Lynne. In September, they also signed a new contract with EMI Records that made provision for records by ELO, which was where their interest now lay. Recruiting the right musicians for gigs would prove an even more lengthy task than the recording of their first album, with over a year elapsing between the first studio sessions and its eventual release.

One group weathered a turbulent year by parting company somewhat acrimoniously in 1969 amid personal and business conflicts, not unlike The Beatles, and then reforming soon afterwards. It helped in that they were brothers. The following summer Barry, Robin and Maurice Gibb, The Bee Gees, settled their differences, and in August, they announced that they 'are there and they will never, ever part again'. Sessions produced an album, *2 Years On* (number 32 in the US), and a new single, 'Lonely Days' (number 33 in the UK, number three in the US).

The hard rock trinity and more

If The Beatles had been the most influential group and the most successful in terms of record sales for much of the 1960s, the act who had the best claim to stealing their crown in 1970 was Led Zeppelin. Formed in 1968 by guitarist Jimmy Page, a former member of The Yardbirds and one of the most in-demand session musicians of all, he had conceived a group who would accomplish as much in the music scene as The Beatles had at their height, yet go about it in a different way. They would keep interviews with the press and television appearances to a minimum and not issue any singles in Britain as they did not wish to become a fly-by-night teen sensation, though they had no control over foreign releases. Their energies would be focused on making music, selling albums and touring. Two or three years previously, Cream had largely created the template by taking blues-rock to a further stage, releasing albums that combined studio and lengthy live cuts, and becoming phenomenally successful in Britain and America, the darlings of the music press – but burning out within a couple of years, largely due to personality conflicts. Page had listened, learnt, and decided that Led Zeppelin would be built to last.

Their second album, *Led Zeppelin II* (number one on both sides of the pond), released at the end of 1969, would be hailed twenty years later by one music historian as 'the musical starting point for heavy metal'. [Waksman, p.263] The album's most well-known track, 'Whole Lotta Love', received airplay almost unprecedented for a piece of music not issued as a single in Britain, or at least not until a limited edition appeared in 1997, long after the group had ceased to exist. (Atlantic Records UK briefly put it out as a single against the wishes of group and management, and some copies reached the shops before it was withdrawn). It was almost a foregone conclusion that somebody would record it. CCS (Collective Consciousness Society), a jazz-rock fusion ensemble consisting of the cream of British session pop, rock and jazz players formed primarily for recording rather than live shows by blues musician Alexis Korner, producer Mickie Most and arranger John Cameron, chose it as their debut single, reaching number thirteen, at the end of the year. It also became the theme music for *Top of the Pops* for the next few years.

Having built themselves a reputation with their first two albums as purveyors for arguably the loudest, fiercest, heaviest rock and blues riffs yet committed to vinyl, it came as a surprise when the third, *Led Zeppelin III* (also number ones in the US and the UK), appeared. Much of it reflected the more blues-based, acoustic side of the group with more folk and Celtic influences, to say nothing of prominent use of acoustic guitars, banjo and mandolin.

If Led Zeppelin were the standard-bearers of hard rock throughout 1970, with their second album the year's top seller in Britain after *Bridge Over Troubled Water*, Deep Purple were close on their heels. Their first three albums in the late 1960s met with little British success, but a change of personnel with new vocalist Ian Gillan and bass guitarist Roger Glover was followed by an upturn in their fortunes. Their roots were in psychedelic rock with occasional influences from the classics, as personified by two of their earliest ventures. *Concerto for Group and Orchestra*, a three-movement epic composed by their keyboard player Jon Lord with lyrics by Gillan, was performed by the group at the Royal Albert Hall, London, with the Royal Philharmonic Orchestra, conducted by Malcolm Arnold, in September 1969, and released as an album three months later (number 26 in the UK). The venture brought them valuable publicity and positive exposure, although Blackmore and Gillan were determined not to be tagged as 'a group who played with orchestras', and were even less enthusiastic about Lord's follow-up, *Gemini Suite*. The first proper rock album by the new line-up, *Deep Purple in Rock*, was released in June 1970 and established them for good (number four in the UK but number 165 in the USA).

Having completed and delivered the album to EMI for release, the management pointed out that there was no obvious single on the album. The group had never thought of themselves as a singles outfit but duly spent an afternoon jamming in the hope of coming across that elusive riff on which a suitable number could be built. Having failed, they went to the pub that evening, and after closing time returned to the studio cheerfully plastered. Blackmore picked up his guitar and began playing the riff from Ricky Nelson's 'Summertime' – and which had also been adapted by The Blues Magoos on 'We Ain't Got Nothin' Yet'. But Purple did have something, which began by Gillan and Glover making up the daftest lyrics they could. For a title, they looked to inspiration from an old jazz tune recorded by Charles Brown twenty years earlier. 'Black Night' was accordingly written, rehearsed, recorded, and released as a single early in June, the same day as the album. Two months later it crawled into the top fifty, and two months after that it peaked at number two in the UK for two weeks, number 66 in the USA two months after that.

The third of 'the trinity of hard rock bands', Black Sabbath, were not far behind. Sometimes called the first true heavy metal outfit, they recorded their debut eponymous album in a single twelve-hour session one day late in 1969, more or less live, and released it the following February to generally negative reviews, but an ecstatic reception from fans who had seen them live (number eight in the UK, 23 in the USA). In September came the second, initially to be called *War Pigs* after the opening track, but changed by Vertigo Records, who feared any controversy arising from fans connecting it with the Vietnam war. Aided by the success of the title track as a single (number four in the UK, 61 in the USA), *Paranoid* (number one in the UK, 12 in the USA) was even more successful. Unashamedly inspired by the opening riff from Led Zeppelin's 'Communication Breakdown', 'Paranoid' was written as an afterthought. They needed a three-minute filler to complete the album, so guitarist Tony Iommi played the riff, and bassist Geezer Butler dashed off a couple of verses about 'getting totally paranoid about people', yet without including the title in the lyrics. Seeing themselves as 'an album band, a more underground band', they found the success of the single a two-edged sword. It led to 'getting screaming kids at gigs, and they just weren't our sort of fans', Iommi said years later to *Kerrang*. 'We didn't want to attract Beatles fans or anything like that. The music was heavy and powerful and we wanted to keep it that way.' [Alexander]

Perhaps the only real rival to all three groups, at least for a while, was Ten Years After. Like Led Zeppelin, their roots were deep in the blues, although they too had a varied palette that enabled them to throw in the occasional surprise with an acoustic number, or one owing more to jazz than rock. An appearance at the Woodstock Festival near New York in August 1969 helped to make them stars in America, while a relentless schedule of gigs and smaller festivals in their native England brought them close to the first division there as well. Sales of their fourth album, *Cricklewood Green* (number four in the UK, 14 in the USA), released in April 1970, was boosted by the appearance of one track, 'Love Like a Man' (a UK number ten), as a single that summer, reaching No. 10.

Also flying the blues-rock banner for a short time were Juicy Lucy, whose turn in the spotlight lasted for two singles, notably an energetic cover of Bo Diddley's 'Who Do You Love' (14 in the UK), and two modestly charting albums during the year. Uriah Heep took a slightly different path, their first album *Very 'Eavy ... Very 'Umble*, treading a path between progressive and hard rock. Though they outlasted many of their contemporaries by years, it was an inauspicious debut panned by many publications at the time, above all *Rolling Stone*, whose reviewer wrote, 'If this group makes it, I'll have to commit suicide. From the first note, you know you don't want to hear any more.' It did, however chart, albeit modestly, in America (at 186).

Throughout the year, various newer rock groups from the other side of the Atlantic also made an impression on the British charts, albeit briefly. The Guess Who, a Canadian quintet, rode high for the first and last time with

'American Woman' (a number one in the USA, number nineteen in Britain), boasting a guitar riff not a million miles removed from 'Whole Lotta Love'. It had been recorded in August 1969, so any suggestions of plagiarising Led Zeppelin (whose musical inspiration had come from Willie Dixon's 'You Need Love') would not have held water. 'American Woman' was criticised by some for being xenophobic, although they immediately denied any such charges. Nevertheless, when invited to play at the White House that summer, Pat Nixon, the President's wife, asked them to omit the song from their set. It was not the last from their guitarist Randy Bachman, who would enjoy even greater success a few years on as leader of Bachman-Turner Overdrive.

Frijid Pink would likewise be one-hit wonders in Britain with their reworking of the old traditional folk song 'House of the Rising Sun', their only top ten hit either side of the Atlantic (number four in the UK, number seven in the USA). Most successful of all were Chicago, initially a prog-jazz rock combo, whose first two hits, 'I'm a Man' (number eight in the UK, US number 49), and '25 or 6 to 4' (number seven in the UK, number four in the USA), were far removed from the more easy listening style which would give them greater hits several years later.

Stars on 45

Most rock groups professed disdain for singles, but unlike Led Zeppelin, most of them bowed to the inevitable. It was apparent to most that issuing a radio-friendly 45 did not necessarily mean selling out to fickle adolescent buyers, and it could often help to create good publicity that all but guaranteed a hit album, as well as *Top of the Pops* appearances. Free had released two albums in 1969 with minor success and were one of several groups gradually building up a reputation through extensive live work, but not every show they played went down a storm.

After a gig at the Durham Students Union building, leaving the stage to the sound of their own footsteps, they realised they needed a really strong number to close the act. Inspiration suddenly struck bassist Andy Fraser, and he started singing 'All Right Now'. He and vocalist Paul Rodgers promptly sat down in the dressing room, and within minutes had the song that would be their breakthrough (Number two in the UK, number four in the USA) and would launch their third album *Fire and Water*. While they would claim it was not typical of their usual style, it became an evergreen rock classic and made four further separate appearances in the British singles chart over the next two decades or so, long after the group had ceased to exist. However, a hastily-recorded and more introspective follow-up album, *Highway* and single, 'The Stealer' (number 49 in the USA), later in the year, failed to consolidate their success, and they disbanded the following year – only to reunite and quickly implode for good a year after that.

The spring and summer months of 1970 demonstrated an eclectic mix of records occupying the British pole position and runner-up. Middle-of-the-road fare, songs that might not have sounded out of place ten years earlier, enjoyed two or more weeks at the summit. Dana's Eurovision Song Contest winner for Ireland, and the England World Cup Squad's singalong 'Back Home' both had a spell No. 1, as did Elvis Presley's schmaltzy 'The Wonder of You', a live version of a hit for Ronnie Hilton in 1959, for six weeks. More noteworthy was Norman Greenbaum's 'Spirit in the Sky', an infectious pop-rock gospelly-flavoured tune skilfully welded to a fuzzbox guitar boogie riff and equally searing rock guitar solo.

Records that stalled at the runner-up position, alongside 'All Right Now', included the one-hit-wonder Northern soul instrumental, 'Groovin'' With Mr Bloe', credited in Britain and America to Cool Heat, to Mr Bloe, a group of session musicians supplying a rhythm section behind the appropriately-named noted harmonica virtuoso Harry Pitch, the experimental 'Neanderthal Man' (22 in the US) by Hotlegs, a trio who would later recruit an additional member and become 10cc, and 'Lola' (a US number nine) by The Kinks, the quite daring-for-its-time tale of a transvestite encounter in Soho.

Progressive rock

Progressive rock boomed throughout the year, and even the less commercially successful names attracted much attention from the critics and media, even if TV appearances and album sales were modest. *Time and a Word*, the second album by Yes, on which the five-piece group were augmented by Royal College of Music students on brass and strings, gave them their album chart debut (number 45 in the UK). Perhaps the greatest media boost for the genre was when Soft Machine, whose style tended more towards modern jazz than most of their peers, were the first rock group invited to play at the annual summer London Promenade Concerts that August. The show was broadcast live on television, although their album *Third* failed to chart. Meanwhile, The Pretty Things, who had started out several years previously as an R'n'B outfit, but gradually changed towards a more psychedelic style, re-established themselves with the album *Parachute*, though in their case, critical acclaim would never be rewarded with commensurate chart success.

More successful were The Nice, a trio whose short existence came to an end that summer with the release of *Five Bridges* (number two in the UK, number 197), containing a live recording of the 'Five Bridges Suite' with the Sinfonia of London Orchestra the previous autumn. Their keyboard player Keith Emerson, regarded by some as the father of progressive rock, lost no time in forming another trio, ELP (Emerson, Lake and Palmer), including ex-King Crimson bassist Greg Lake and ex-Crazy World of Arthur Brown and Atomic Rooster drummer Carl Palmer. They played their debut gigs that August, including the Isle of Wight Festival, before releasing their self-titled debut album in December (number four in the UK, number 18 in the USA). Looking back over forty years later, he recalled that when he was in The Nice and then in the early days of ELP, nobody had ever heard of progressive music. Palmer told Malcolm Dome: 'What we did had some jazz in it, a little blues and also had the classical references. It was only later on that people began to call our music 'progressive', and that's when the genre began to grow. With hindsight, I'd say that ELP were the pioneers of progressive rock.' For a while, the story went round that Jimi Hendrix was going to join the trio on guitar – until it was revealed as a joke. Any such band would have been called HELP.

King Crimson weathered the loss of their bassist, as they did many other personnel changes throughout their career, spending several weeks in the album chart that summer with their second effort, *In the Wake of Poseidon* (number four in the UK, number 31 in the USA). It more than compensated for the fate of their single 'Cat Food', which flopped despite appearing on *TOTP* in March. Nevertheless, several rock groups still took the Led Zeppelin 'no singles' route. Forcing fans to spend two pounds on an album rather than ten shillings (50 pence) on a single meant more money to swell the coffers, and there was always the risk of being dismissed as teenybopper fare if forced into releasing commercial pop songs aimed squarely at a mainly teenage audience. One of the few progressive acts equally at home in both charts were Family, who straddled blues, jazz, folk, country and hard rock. Fronted by Roger Chapman, of the distinctive gravelly voice and vibrato, and guitarist Charlie Whitney, they scored consistently throughout the year with 'Weaver's Answer' (11), *A Song for Me* (number four), and *Anyway* (number seven in the UK, number 28 in the USA).

Make love, not war – or protest

The mantra 'make love, not war', 'give peace a chance', and protests against the continuing war in Vietnam, were much in vogue in Britain and America as the old decade merged into the new, although reflected but little among the music fraternity in Britain. The song 'Get Together', written some five years earlier by Chet Powers, with its message to 'try to love one another right now', was recorded by several acts during the next few years, sometimes as 'Let's Get Together'. The most successful versions were by The Youngbloods in America in 1969, and (as 'Everybody Get Together'), the last of several major British hits by The Dave Clark Five a year later (a UK number eight). It was a sentiment reflected in a similarly-titled song that also underwent changes over time, Wilbert Harrison's early 1960s 'Let's Stick Together', rejigged and renamed 'Let's Work Together' by him in 1970, and more successfully by Canned Heat (number two in the UK, 26 in the USA).

Apart from Jimmy Cliff's 'Vietnam' (number 46), the British charts featured little in the way of obvious protest songs. Some found a subtle way to express their feelings, perhaps none better than The Moody Blues, who had established themselves as one of the leading lights of prog rock, with a style that relied partly on semi-classical arrangements using mellotron, synthesisers and flute. One of their earlier albums had been in effect a collaboration with the London Festival Orchestra, though the group maintained control of the project.

Listening to the news one evening about the ongoing conflict on the other side of the world, vocalist and guitarist Justin Hayward was angry. The only reason to have a war to him, he said, was to do with starvation, and people fighting for their lives. 'But just for a bit of territory, a bit of land somewhere, was stupid. In my own naive way, I put a lot of those feelings into ['Question'].' Inspired by the feeling of unrest prevalent in America, he combined two separate pieces, an up-tempo riff followed by a slower, dreamier segment, into a song lasting almost six minutes, dominated by 12-string acoustic guitars, frantic drumming and equally dramatic vocal harmonies at the forefront. The resulting epic 'Question' (number two in the UK, number six in the USA) was more complex than the average chart single. His basic idea in writing it, Hayward explained, was that 'after a decade of peace and love, it still seemed we hadn't made a difference in 1970. I suppose that was the theme of the song.' [Reed, interview] It spawned an even higher-charting album, *A Question of Balance* (number one in the UK, number three in the USA).

Just as irritated with the world about them, while less subtle and less successful, were The Edgar Broughton Band. They attracted controversy through staging free gigs at places like children's playgrounds and circumventing local council bans by playing from the back of a flat-bed lorry. At one show, the audience vandalised the venue with paint supplied to them by the band. Broughton admitted afterwards that he had given it to the punters, defending himself by saying that 'we didn't tell them to do anything with it'. Their main chart achievements that year were 'Out Demons Out' (39 in the UK), an adaptation of the Fugs' incendiary 'Exorcising the Demons Out of the Pentagon', and an album *Sing Brother Sing*. Less successful was one of the few openly political singles of the year, 'Up Yours!', released at the time of the general election in June 1970, a rallying call to drop out and refuse to vote for anyone. It was wholeheartedly punk in spirit, if not in the singalong waltz-tempo and the frenzied arrangement of strings behind the out of tune vocals and raspberries.

The climate of protest was reflected loud and clear in some of the music from America. Thinly-veiled anger was present in several songs from Creedence Clearwater Revival, at that time among the most consistently successful singles and albums bands on both sides of the Atlantic. 'Fortunate Son', a single early in the year from their album *Willy and the Poor Boys*, waved a fist at 'rich men making war and poor men having to fight them'. John Fogerty, the group's front man and writer, said in his memoirs that it was his comment on the privileged sons of senators and congressmen who were given a deferment from the military forces, or else a choice position in the army.

Singer-songwriters
When Bob Dylan first became a worldwide success in the mid-1960s, he had been hailed as the one protest singer to become a household name and a big name in music. By 1970, he astonished everyone with his most bizarre record

yet, *Self Portrait*. A 24-track double album, it contained only eight numbers written by the artist himself (four of them live recordings of old songs from his Isle of Wight Festival appearance in 1969, two instrumentals, and a two-line chant sung entirely by two female backing vocalists), alongside numbers made famous by the Everly Brothers, Gordon Lightfoot, Simon & Garfunkel, and easy listening standards like 'Blue Moon'. Most reviews at the time were merciless, Greil Marcus of *Rolling Stone* opening his with the words, 'What is this shit?' Opinions have mellowed over the years, yet such was Dylan's selling power that it still sold heavily (number one in the UK, number four in the USA). Yet looking back on it in interviews about fifteen years later, he admitted that it was a bit of a joke. 'I wish these people would just forget about me,' he said, reported in C. Heylin's *Dylan Behind the Shades*. 'I wanna do something they can't possibly like, they can't relate to. They'll see it, and they'll listen, and they'll say, 'Well, let's get on to the next person. He ain't sayin' it no more. He ain't givin' us what we want.'' Yet as if to reconnect with his audience, he followed it up in November with *New Morning*, which had the virtue of being completely self-penned. However, apart from the much-covered 'If Not for You', the album boasted few memorable songs, but still flew out of the shops (number one in the UK, number seven in the USA).

His influence continued to spread far and wide and on few individuals more than Van Morrison. According to his wife Janet, 'he thought Dylan was the only contemporary worthy of his attention'. His music drew from many genres, from pop, soul, jazz and Irish folk. Like Dylan, he would release two albums in 1970, with *Moondance* (a UK number 32, 29 in the US) in January and *His Band and the Street Choir* (which reached number 18 in the UK, 32 in the US) in November.

Others were more than happy to assume the protest mantle and confront authority by drawing attention to contemporary injustice, environmental concerns, and their anger with Vietnam. The mood in traditionally conservative America was very volatile at that time. Rock musicians with shoulder-length hair and beards were beloved by the alienated student generation but reviled as hippies by the rest. As one of the British group's biographers observed, in such a climate of unrest and fear, 'rock concerts like Led Zeppelin's grope-feasts were considered a public danger and a needless excuse to get an already excitable youth population *really* riled up'.

One group who tapped into this mood were Crosby, Stills, Nash and Young. On 4 May, a contingent of Ohio National Guard officers shot and killed four students at Kent State University during a demonstration against the continuing south-east Asian conflict. Incandescent after reading a magazine report of the incident, Neil Young picked up his guitar and wrote the song 'Ohio', a fierce indictment that mentioned President Richard Nixon by name in the first line of the lyrics, and repeated the line 'Four dead in Ohio' several times. Calling out the President as directly as that, Crosby commented, was 'the bravest thing I ever heard'. The song was recorded just seventeen days after the shootings, and rush-released as a single in June, with an equally uncompromising number on the B-side, Stills's 'The Cost of Freedom'. Banned by several AM radio stations across the United States, it was heavily played on underground FM stations in larger cities and college towns, and charted at number 14, though it made little impact in Britain.

Nevertheless, *Déjà Vu*, the album that had preceded it in March, would mark the pinnacle of their success. The first album they recorded as a quartet (their 1969 debut having been made by the trio before Young joined), it was easily the best-selling of their career (a number five in the UK, number one in the USA). It came in a striking sleeve designed to look like an old leatherbound book, bearing an ersatz-19th century photo of all six members (including bassist Greg Reeves and drummer Dallas Taylor) in Old West garb, and a dog that wandered into camera view, that had to be mounted by hand on the front. Like The Beatles, all four members released solo albums, though Young was by far the most successful, with *After the Gold Rush* becoming a transatlantic top ten album.

It was definitely Joni Mitchell's year as well. Previously known mainly on the strength of her haunting 'Both Sides Now', a hit for Judy Collins (number 14 in the UK in 1970, it had already been a number eight in the US in 1968), and recorded by many others including Neil Diamond, Frank Sinatra and Bing Crosby, she became recognised as a singer-songwriter in her own right, not just for her 1970 album *Ladies of the Canyon* (number eight in the UK, 27 in the USA), and 'Woodstock', but also for another number on the same album, 'Big Yellow Taxi'.

On 16 October 1970, she headlined a benefit concert, 'Amchitka', at the Pacific Coliseum, Vancouver, on a bill that also included Phil Ochs and James Taylor. The event was to draw attention to fund Greenpeace's protests at the testing of nuclear weapons by the U.S. Atomic Energy Commission at Amchitka, Alaska. The concert raised $17,164 in what turned out to be Greenpeace's first significant protest, although due to delays in obtaining copyright clearances and adequate tape restoration, the subsequent live album, *Amchitka*, was not released until nearly forty years later.

James Taylor, who was briefly Mitchell's boyfriend, proved to be one of the major discoveries of the year. Having come from America to Britain the previous decade, he became the first American artist to be signed to the Beatles' Apple label, yet his debut self-titled album made little impression. Returning home, he signed to Warner Brothers, and his second album *Sweet Baby James*, which went top ten in America and Britain, launched him at the forefront of contemporary singer-songwriters, thanks to its best-known song, 'Fire and Rain' (number 42 in the UK, number three in the USA).

In Britain, the nearest equivalent to an acoustic-based singer-songwriter was Cat Stevens. Although he had always written his own material, as well as penning hits for several other acts, he had ploughed a more commercial pop furrow in 1967, before a bout of tuberculosis stopped him in his tracks. His re-emergence in 1970 with *Mona Bone Jakon* and single, 'Lady D'Arbanville' (a UK number eight), revealed a very different figure. By the end of the year, he had followed it up with *Tea for the Tillerman* (20 in the UK, eight in the USA). Coincidentally, it appeared the same month as the American release (appearing in Britain the following spring) of another London-born singer-songwriter, *The Man Who Sold the World* by David Bowie. Having made his mark with a solitary 1969 top ten hit, 'Space Oddity', Bowie would remain a little-known figure for another year or so, before becoming arguably the most influential solo artist in Britain for many years until his death in 2016. A group who would soon owe much to his support (and one of his songs), Mott the Hoople, seen as a combination of the Rolling Stones and Dylan, had made their presence felt with the dark, brooding album *Mad Shadows*. Their greatest days were to come.

Meanwhile, if Bowie had a rival, it was Elton John, whose second, self-titled album earlier that year (number five in the UK, six in the US), quickly followed by his third, *Tumbleweed Connection* (number two in the UK, five in the USA), would help kick-start a very long career. Another artist aiming for a similar audience was Gilbert O'Sullivan, known initially for his unique visual image of cloth cap, short trousers and pudding basin haircut. Yet his first single at the end of the year gave proof of a remarkable talent that would bring him chart-topping singles in Britain, Europe and America. 'Nothing Rhymed' (a UK number eight), which he said was his way of saying that things were out of order in the world, had been inspired by watching footage on television of starving children in Africa.

Around the same time, the largely acoustic duo, Tyrannosaurus Rex, having long had a cult following, gave a taste of things to come. Shortening their name to T. Rex, they followed a few minor successes with a major hit at last in 'Ride a White Swan' (a UK number two). During what one commentator called the 'treading-water year' of 1970, with most major groups recently splitting up or ailing, and supergroups lacking the gang bond to make them last, and the search for a seventies sound, it would be T. Rex who were poised to kick-start the new era of pop. Within a year, they expanded to a quartet, to become briefly, the biggest-selling group in Britain.

Folk-rock, jazz-rock and other fusions

Folk-rock was a broad church that straddled the domain of the singer-songwriter as well as traditional musicians who were prepared to embrace a more contemporary setting that would help him, her or them break out of the purist folk-club straitjacket. Regarded as the founding fathers of the genre, Fairport Convention had formed about three years later, with a repertoire that embraced the songs of Dylan, Leonard Cohen and their ilk, as well as adaptations of English traditional song over the centuries, with an ever-changing personnel that rarely remained unaltered for two consecutive albums. One of their early members, Iain Matthews, had left to form his own group, Matthews Southern

Comfort, whose chart success was limited to one solitary single, their version of Joni Mitchell's 'Woodstock' (a UK number one, although only number 23 in the US). More recently, former vocalist Sandy Denny had also departed to form Fotheringay, who recorded and released one widely-acclaimed but poorly-selling album. They began a second that remained unfinished when she split for a solo career (later to rejoin Fairport), and they disbanded.

Another of their founding members, Ashley Hutchings, had left in 1969 to form his own outfit, Steeleye Span. The rest of the line-up comprised two duos, Gay and Terry Woods, and Tim Hart and Maddy Prior. As a group, they would likewise have a lengthy career, recording mostly traditional folk song with an electric punch that occasionally offended the more purist elements, punctuated with ever-changing personnel over the years. Their debut, *Hark! The Village Wait*, was released in the spring of 1970, after the Woods had departed, leaving the others unsure as to whether they still had a group or not. Maddy Prior would continue to front them, with the occasional short break, for some fifty years (and counting).

Treading a slightly different path were Pentangle, more a fusion of folk, jazz and blues. They were fronted by vocalist Jacqui McShee and guitarists Bert Jansch and John Renbourn, long regarded as two of the finest musicians in their genre. Their second album *Basket of Light* (reaching number five in the UK), was a steady seller throughout the year, while they also enjoyed modest success with a single, 'Light Flight', the theme for TV drama series *Take Three Girls*.

By contrast, an act that had the briefest of careers was The Humblebums, a Scottish duo comprising what seemed an unlikely pairing of Gerry Rafferty, a reclusive singer-songwriter, and future stand-up comic Billy Connolly. An album, *Open Up the Door*, preceded by a single, 'Shoeshine Boy', only sold to the faithful. They parted company soon afterwards, but audiences would hear much of both in years to come.

More built to last were Lindisfarne, a Tyneside quintet named after the Holy Island off the northeast coast. Their influences were drawn from pop, various folk, blues, and even soul influences. A combination of the writing talents of singer-guitarist Alan Hull, bass player and violinist Rod Clements, plus a wealth of multi-instrumental skills, contributed to their debut album that November, *Nicely Out of Tune* (number eight in the UK later in 1972). At a time when some were still looking for a 'new Beatles', for a while, they seemed to fit the bill, a few even dubbing them 'the folk-rock Beatles'. Like Fairport and Steeleye, they would disband once or twice, but were still recording and gigging well into the 21st century.

Folk music sometimes extended its long arm into other genres. Traffic, one of the most eclectic names of all with their fusion of pop, rock, jazz and psychedelia that was impossible to pigeonhole, had briefly split, but reunited in 1970 when front man Steve Winwood, having helped form the shortlived Blind Faith in 1969, started to record a solo album. The project morphed into a Traffic reunion, with a new album *John Barleycorn Must Die* (a UK number

31

eleven and a US number five), its title track an old traditional English folk song of which variations would be recorded by many other contemporary performers.

Sharing some common musical ground with a refreshing flavour of folk, rock, and an ear for instantly infectious songs, were McGuinness Flint, led by former Manfred Mann guitarist Tom McGuinness, former John Mayall's Bluesbreakers drummer Hughie Flint, and enriched – for their first releases – by the duo Benny Gallagher and Graham Lyle, who had previously been signed as songwriters by The Beatles' Apple label to provide material for some of their artists. The first, and most successful result of their work together, was a classic single, 'When I'm Dead and Gone' (a UK number two, also reaching 47 in the USA), an irresistible folk-rock singalong with mandolin centre-stage. The original Manfred Mann group had disbanded in 1969, with two members, leader and keyboard player Manfred Mann himself, and Mike Hugg, who had switched from drums to vocals and electric piano. After having been a dependable hit single machine for the second half of the 1960s, much to their frustration, they formed the more experimental jazz-rock outfit Manfred Mann Chapter III. Two albums and a single, 'Happy Being Me', received little exposure and passed largely unnoticed. Colosseum, formed by drummer Jon Hiseman and saxophonist Dick Heckstall-Smith, were almost unique among jazz-rock combos in riding high with two albums that year, *Valentyne Suite* (15 in the UK) and *Daughter of Time* (reaching 23), without the launchpad of a chart single, but the more commercial CCS apart, jazz-rock still remained largely a minority taste.

McGuinness Flint were among several who admitted that among their foremost influences was the music of The Band, an American-Canadian group who had originally been Dylan's backing band on tour, before becoming a recording entity in their own right. Their music was hard to classify, taking elements of Americana, rock, folk, R'n'B country and jazz. With such an eclectic mix, several names on both sides of the Atlantic would also look to them for inspiration. Another was Eric Clapton, one of Britain's most highly respected guitarists, yet the most reluctant of stars, who had become frustrated as a member of his previous groups, Cream and Blind Faith, and longed to be just one in a larger band where he was no longer given front billing. Initially, playing for fun with Delaney and Bonnie and Friends gave him renewed enthusiasm for his music. In 1970, he recorded his first, eponymous solo album with their backing band, plus American session musicians including Leon Russell and Stephen Stills, and it reached number 14. Next, he put together a new group, Derek and the Dominos, using some of the same musicians, to record the album *Layla and Other Assorted Love Songs* (a lowly 68 in the UK 16 in the US), which sold few copies at the time, but was with hindsight recognised as a classic.

Though it might have been a lean time for one of Britain's most respected guitarists, another was about to reap the rewards of having paid his dues for some years. Since 1963, the Christmas No. 1 single had generally been either a Beatles single or a novelty tune. 1970 broke the mould with Dave Edmunds and his revival of an old 1950s rock'n'roll hit for Smiley Lewis, 'I Hear You Knocking' (a UK number one and also a US number four). Though the record was credited to Dave Edmunds Rockpile, which was basically a revolving door name for any musicians he was working with, it featured him as a one-man band responsible for most if not all vocals and instruments.

Tamla Motown, soul and reggae

The wind of change also came to Tamla Motown, which had until then been synonymous with infectious, danceable pop that rarely if ever carried any message, and was to a certain extent finely crafted by production teams of songwriters, session musicians and in-house producers. By 1970, some of its artists were keen to exert more control over their work in musical and lyrical terms. Stevie Wonder's *Signed, Sealed, Delivered* (a number 25 hit in the USA) was hailed by some as the best soul album of the year, finding him increasingly involved in not only writing or co-writing the songs but also in co-producing them.

Other Motown artists were also beginning to release songs that reflected the mood of the times. Marvin Gaye issued 'Abraham, Martin and John' (a UK number nine), written by Dick Holler, and originally an American top ten hit for Dion in 1968. It paid tribute to the memory of Abraham Lincoln, Martin Luther King, and John Kennedy (and by implication Bobby Kennedy as well), icons of social change who were all assassinated. It signified a complete change in direction for Gaye.

Also reflecting the prevailing mood was a single by The Temptations. 'Ball of Confusion (That's What the World Is Today)', a big hit in both the UK and the USA, also addressed the woes of the world – 'Segregation, determination, demonstration, integration, aggravation, humiliation, obligation to our nation – the cities ablaze in the summertime'. Even more to the point was another song they had recorded, a polemic on the Vietnam conflict, 'War', co-written and produced by Norman Whitfield as an album track. Company founder Berry Gordy Jr. had initially told his in-house songwriters not to focus on controversial subjects, but some were prepared to disregard his ruling, and Motown could hardly ignore demands for it to be issued as a single. As The Temptations were at the time the label's most popular group, both company and group were reluctant to antagonise what was assumed to be their rather more conservative fan base. Whitfield knew the song was too good to let pass as a mere album track and decided to re-record it with someone who had less to lose. Edwin Starr, a recent Motown signing with only one hit to his name so far, was prepared and also eager to take the risk, and the bosses bowed to public demand. His recording of 'War' (a US number one and a number three in the UK), a masterpiece of controlled anger, proved one of the reluctant company's great success stories of the year.

It came at a time when most of their other acts were playing safe with relatively innocuous fare. Diana Ross and The Supremes had parted company early that year, with both Ross and her former group enjoying further transatlantic hits. So did The Four Tops, while leaving their more pop-dance days behind, moving into sophisticated soul territory with fare like 'Still Water (Love)' and a revival of 'It's All in the Game' recorded by several others since being written in 1951 (and surely the only No. 1 song ever co-written by a one-time American Vice-President, Charles G. Dawes).

For a few years, the label had fared well, particularly in Britain, by reissuing oldies that sold better the second time around. In 1970 they took this process one stage further when a remixed version of 'Tears of a Clown' by Smokey Robinson and The Miracles, previously a little-known 1967 album track, was issued as a single by the British arm of Tamla Motown Records and subsequently in America (number one in both the UK and the USA). Meanwhile, that year the label made a new family group, The Jackson 5, the year's most successful new act in America. Their first four singles, including 'I Want You Back' and 'I'll Be There', all reached number one, and made the British top ten. Motown's most consistent solo performer in Britain during the year was Jimmy Ruffin. Always much more successful there than in America, he scored three British top ten entries, one, 'I'll Say Forever My Love', being a reissue that had failed to chart on initial release two years earlier.

Although the label might break new ground with some artists as well as mining its back catalogue to maximum effect, it had lost its best songwriting partnership, which felt inadequately rewarded by the management and left to found a rival organisation. For several years, the cream of Motown hits had been written by the trio of Brian and Eddie Holland and Lamont Dozier. In 1969 they established two new labels, Invictus and Hot Wax. Facing legal action from Motown supremo, Berry Gordy Jr, they were temporarily prevented from releasing any of their own compositions on record. To circumvent this, they wrote and released material which was jointly credited to Ron Dunbar, one of their producers, and the non-existent Edyth Wayne.

A stream of successes on both outlets followed. By early autumn 1970, two Dunbar-Wayne credits, Freda Payne's 'Band of Gold' (a UK number one and a US number three), and Chairmen of the Board's 'Give Me Just a Little More Time' (number three in both territories) both rode high. Another song written by Dunbar and Chairmen of the Board's vocalist General Johnson, 'Patches', was not only recorded by the latter, but also became one of the greatest soul hits of the year, top five in both the UK and the USA, when covered by Clarence Carter. He had long been a household name in America and one of the mainstays of the Atlantic label, but this would be his only British success in a lengthy career.

Even though it failed to catch on in America for a while, reggae was one of the great success stories in Britain in 1970. The way had been paved in the previous decade, mainly by Jamaican singer Desmond Dekker, who, after a number one with 'Israelites' in 1969, consolidated his success the next year with 'You Can Get It If You Really Want' (a UK number two), written by Jimmy Cliff, one of the major writers and singers in the genre. Cliff's greatest hit of the year was with 'Wild World' (a UK number eight), a song written by Cat Stevens. Stevens' own recording became a Top 20 single in America. The oddest history for a reggae hit in Britain came at the start of the year, with the instrumental 'Elizabethan Reggae', a new version of the light orchestral work composed by Ronald Binge nearly twenty years earlier. For its first few weeks of sale, it was wrongly credited to the producer, Byron Lee, before being corrected to the name of the actual performer, Boris Gardiner.

That summer, a record that came close to reggae, 'Love Is Life', would launch the career of Hot Chocolate, a multi-racial group based in Britain, fronted by Jamaican-born vocalist Errol Brown. With their remarkable ability to embrace a wealth of genres, and their ability to touch on subjects such as racism, as well as standard boy and girl lyrics in their music, they would be the only group to have at least one hit single in Britain every year until 1986. During the year, their songwriting partnership, comprising Brown and the group's bassist Tony Wilson, also provided top thirty hits for other acts, namely 'Think About Your Children' for Mary Hopkin, 'Bet Yer Life I Do' for Herman's Hermits, and 'Heaven Is Here' for Julie Felix. Looking back on his career shortly before his farewell tour in 2009, Brown looked back on how the group had been pioneers in introducing pop, rock, soul and funk into their music. If your music was neither soul nor rock, he said, 'people had a problem knowing where to put you … We basically wanted to be real, and progress as artists, and though we were a little bit ahead of our time, we still made it, because the songs themselves were emotionally truthful and people connected with them.' As The Hot Chocolate Band, the group had achieved their first big break through recording their own reggae version of 'Give Peace a Chance', as John Lennon had heard a demo, loved it and issued it as a one-off on the Apple label.

The Beatles: Unfinished business

Elsewhere, the shadows of the no longer Fab Four still loomed large, no longer collectively, but individually. At the end of the year, Lennon's harrowing, confessional album, *John Lennon/Plastic Ono Band* was anything but commercial, but still sold healthily (number eight in the UK, number six in the US). Ringo Starr's second solo album, *Beaucoups of Blues*, a collection of country songs recorded in Nashville, attracted less interest and modest sales, reaching only 65 in the US. Meanwhile, their erstwhile lead guitarist, often dubbed 'The Quiet One', was recording what would come to be recognised by some as the best solo Beatles album ever.

George Harrison had been the first to release any solo material, restricted so far to two avant-garde experimental albums the previous decade. He had particularly enjoyed the freedom of being able to collaborate with other musicians outside the group, and perhaps never more than when he had visited Bob Dylan that May in New York. A more or less spontaneous session was hastily convened for both songwriters, aided by musicians Charlie Daniels on bass and Russ Kunkel on drums. Between them, they rattled off a selection of standards, like 'All I Have To Do Is Dream', 'Cupid', 'Ghost Riders in the Sky', plus The Beatles' 'Yesterday' and Dylan's own 'Rainy Day Women # 12 and 35'. The only brief reference in conversation to the guitarist's former group came when he turned to Daniels and joked 'You want to be a Beatle?'

His first proper mainstream solo album, recorded that summer and autumn, would be the triple album *All Things Must Pass*. Phil Spector was called in to co-produce, but after a few weeks, his legendary unpredictable behaviour proved his downfall. After bringing a gun into the studios, leaving it in full view on the recording console, and hurting his arm when he fell drunkenly off a chair, an angry Harrison told him his services were no longer required and completed the production duties himself.

Meanwhile, the group who still dominated the music scene, even though they were no longer together, still had unfinished business. On 31 December 1970, McCartney filed a lawsuit in the High Court to dissolve The Beatles' partnership. He claimed that The Beatles had ceased to perform together as a group, so the purpose of their partnership was no more; that the other three members had appointed Allen Klein as their business manager, despite his (McCartney's) opposition and in breach of their partnership agreement, and that he had never been given the audited accounts during the four years of their partnership for which he had asked. It helped to serve as final confirmation, if any was needed, that the dream was over and that 1970 had ushered in a new era.

Conclusion

So, did 1970 mark a decisive break from the 1960s? Was it a case of 'out with the old, in with the new?' It was noticed that of all acts who had number one singles in Britain during the previous decade, only Elvis Presley attained the same feat in 1970 – and nobody topped the chart more than once all year. Cliff Richard, the nearest British equivalent to Elvis, would enjoy one solitary top ten hit in his own country that year, while two of the other most consistent soloists in Britain during the 1960s, both long-established favourites with the housewives' generation, Tom Jones and Cilla Black, were also about to find the going more tough than formerly. Frank Sinatra achieved a record of sorts when 'My Way', a top-five hit in 1969, stayed in the Top 50 for all but eight weeks of 1970, never climbing higher than 24 in the UK. 1960s evergreens The Beach Boys found success with an old recording of the traditional 'Cottonfields' (a UK number five), but their more adventurous new album *Sunflower* (29 in the UK, a lowly 151 in the USA) sold less well, despite enthusiastic reviews, and they would never regain their earlier high profile.

It was certainly a new beginning for some, in that The Beatles and Simon and Garfunkel were not the only front-rank names to go their own separate ways.

As Richard Williams noted in *The Times* at the end of the year, pop music – or rather fans – had long taken it for granted that groups would stay together, and there was a general assumption that they would remain as units forever. The first months of 1970 had seen the first change in this attitude, 'mainly from the musicians, although the public is beginning to catch on to the concept that musicians can leave one context and go on to greater things in another'. [Williams]

At the same time, Jon Landau observed in *Rolling Stone* that 'as we move into a new decade and the Beatles recede into our musical past, one gets the sense we are moving into a new, constructive period of transition – a prelude to some new approach to music in the Seventies.' Part of the new approach was that members of established groups could record solo albums or collaborate with others, without leaving their main outfit. 'The group? We're still friends,' Stephen Stills told *The Times* in December. 'I don't want to get myself locked into one thing.' In fact, he had been fired by Crosby, Nash and Young during their tour in July, and then almost immediately reinstated for the remaining dates, but they disbanded immediately afterwards. After a spate of recording solo albums, they continued to collaborate in various permutations and reunite, still bickering, some three years later. Very rock'n'roll.

While it is always easier to look back at specific dates or eras in hindsight, some people recognised at the time that the atmosphere seemed different. Richard DiLello, a former employee at the Beatles' Apple press office, decided to become a photographer, and at a London gig later that year took some shots of Black Sabbath and Emerson, Lake & Palmer. At once, he realised that music was changing radically. 'It was a very different vibe from what the Beatles had given off. I thought we were entering a darker period.' His mood might have been influenced by three recent unexpected deaths of renowned musicians and performers within the space of a month, those of Jimi Hendrix, Janis Joplin, and Al Wilson of Canned Heat, all at the early age of 27. (The previous year, Brian Jones of the Rolling Stones had died at the same age, all four of them being what the media would later come to speak of in later years as 'the 27 club'). There was a palpable sense of loss when Hendrix died. Eric Clapton later recalled in his memoirs that he saw a white left-handed Stratocaster on sale in the West End of London. On impulse, he bought it to give him as a present as he was going to see Sly and the Family Stone at the Lyceum, and Jimi would surely be there. He never turned up, and Clapton only heard next day. He said in his autobiography: 'I felt incredibly upset and very angry, and was filled with a feeling of terrible loneliness.'

The old underground was the new mainstream, the singles chart no longer almost exclusively made up of pop, straightforward rock'n'roll and easy listening. In the wake of shows at the Isle of Wight and Woodstock, festivals also became more than an occasional event. While they might have often run at a heavy financial loss for the organisers, and often provoked the wrath of local community groups and authorities who sought to regulate if not ban them

1970: the year rock became mainstream

altogether, they were here to stay. Nobody could foresee how the modestly-titled Pop, Folk and Blues Festival at Worthy Farm, near Shepton Mallet in Somerset that September, where an audience of 1,500 paid £1 to see a bill including Tyrannosaurus Rex, Al Stewart, Quintessence and Stackridge, would grow into the national institution that became Glastonbury.

Several pop bands came of age, while heavy and progressive rock became more commercially acceptable. So did reggae and ska, which shook off the taint of being novelty music with its main artists being nine-day wonders. More rock, folk and soul acts, not just the few hardcore protest folk singers, directly addressed political, anti-war themes in their music, and did not shy away from political comment at the risk of alienating their less conservative fans (or rather, not all of them). Making a record that risked being banned by radio stations need not be a death blow, and sometimes a little controversy was good publicity – which, far from harming the chances of a single, could result in curiosity, and thus better sales than if it was heard regularly on the airwaves. Growing anger with American involvement in Vietnam was a catalyst to some, even if initially lost on many a British artist. Pete Townshend would recall his shame after being asked to record a radio commercial urging listeners to join the U.S. airforce, before The Who played a gig at an airforce base in 1970. 'Young Americans were concerned about being blown to bits in Vietnam and I, a naïve English twit, came prancing over hot on the heels of The Beatles and Herman's Hermits to make my fortune and bring it back to Britain.'

A few artists who took their bow would shortly become major names. Marc Bolan of Tyrannosaurus Rex, soon to become T. Rex, would experience a meteoric rise as the nation's top pin-up, followed by an equally meteoric fall and partial recovery before his untimely death. Rod Stewart, frontman of The Faces, would leave his group behind and become unstoppable, as would singer-songwriter Elton John. Michael Jackson of the Jackson 5, aged only eleven when 'I Want You Back' topped the American charts in January, would also go solo and become the self-proclaimed king of pop, responsible for the multi-million selling *Thriller*. Status Quo, makers of two middling-sized hit singles in 1970, would become one of Britain's most durable groups. The Bee Gees, who had risen and fallen in the 1960s, would have one of the most chequered careers of all, and only the deaths of two of the three members, nine years apart, would bring their story to a close.

Finally, by the end of 1970, it was becoming the age of band members' solo projects; bootleggers were encouraging more and more acts to issue live albums, and studio albums were becoming more like works of art, regularly appearing in gatefold sleeves, sometimes with posters, lyric inserts or booklets and other enclosed or attached memorabilia. As Landau had remarked, everyone and everything had begun moving into a new, constructive period of transition.

25 significant albums of 1970

It goes without saying that many of us would find it almost impossible to limit such a selection to only 25. I have aimed for a representative choice from different genres, including the great and the very good, the obvious huge sellers that could not be omitted, and one or two of the sometimes overlooked. All are given approximately in order of British release.

Each has been subsequently remastered and reissued on CD, sometimes double, triple or even quadruple, with additional tracks. These reviews are basically of the original 1970 British vinyl releases, with reference to bonus tracks in certain cases.

Moondance – Van Morrison

Personnel:
Van Morrison: lead vocals, guitar, harmonica
John Platania: guitar
Jeff Labes: keyboards
Jack Schroer: saxophones
Colin Tilton: flute, saxophone
John Klingberg: bass
Gary Mallaber: drums, percussion
Produced at A & R Studios, New York, August-December 1969 by Van Morrison and
Lewis Merenstein.
UK release date: February 1970. US release date: January 1970
Record label: Warner Bros
Highest chart places: UK: 32 US: 29
Running time: 38:14
All songs written by Van Morrison.

Van Morrison's first album of the decade was the third in his lengthy solo
career. Although the title track was never a hit, and not released as a single for
seven years (and even then only in America), it has grown in stature and long
been acclaimed as one of his most popular and distinctive numbers. As a result,
it has tended to overshadow the rest of one of the most consistent and highly
regarded records he ever made.

Morrison had written all the songs for the album on acoustic guitar, and
recruited a group of musicians with whom he had never worked before.
After he had jammed with them, they went into the studio with no written
arrangements, allowing the songs to take shape and fall into place almost
spontaneously. The end result is an almost carefree collection in which he
drew on his influences from several different genres, from jazz and soul to pop-
rock, gospel and folk.

Taken as a whole, the record is alternately light, dark, always focused and
without any two tracks sounding really similar. Above all, it has a timeless
quality and never sounds in the least dated. On some of his subsequent
albums, Morrison would become known for long, rambling tracks, but on this
one everything is kept short and sweet, with only one number just breaking the
five-minute barrier. In most recent online polls of 'Van Morrison albums ranked
best to worst', *Moondance* comes out second, beaten only by its predecessor
Astral Weeks.

'And It Stoned Me'

Despite its title, the opening track has no drug connotations. Van later said that
it recalled an encounter during his childhood. When he was twelve, he and
a friend went out fishing one day. On their way back they stopped at a small
stone cottage to ask an old man 'with the sunshine in his eyes' for a drink of

water, and he gave them some from a nearby stream. As they drank from it together, it was as if time stood still for him. For five minutes everything was quiet and he felt as if he was in this 'other dimension'. With a measured, stately feel – and, in places, a similar chord sequence – evoking the mood of The Band's 'The Weight' – he muses on how the occasion 'stoned me to my soul', with piano prominent throughout, plus fills from saxophone and his own acoustic guitar break.

'Moondance'

The title track, which has received regular airplay as an album track down the ages, is almost too familiar to need much introduction, as a song partly about the joys of autumn as the leaves are falling, partly about the thrills of making love. It finds Morrison exploring his jazz roots with a song built largely on piano chords, a walking bass pattern, and a soft shuffling touch on the drums, mostly from the brushes. Saxophone and flute add to the overall colour, as he sings with a spring in his step of 'a fantabulous night to make romance 'neath the cover of October skies'. It has been covered by several other artists including Georgie Fame, Michael Bublé, and Ramsey Lewis with Nancy Wilson.

'Crazy Love'

A similar feeling of romance pervades this slower number. It has something of the feel of a Motown ballad, with high-pitched vocals accompanied by the backing singers who provide a gospel tinge and a low-key acoustic mood, supported by an unobtrusively gentle rhythm section.

'Caravan'

A mid-tempo pace is the order for this soulful song, characterised by rippling piano and sturdy sax playing, for a song that equates the nostalgia of listening to the radio with a group of friends, all in an imaginary caravan. Or is it a group of dancing girls, personified by the mysterious barefooted gypsy player who performs around the campfire? Alternatively, is this caravan a metaphor for a journey through life, as it has all his friends aboard, people who will stay with him until the end? Whatever the meaning is, it conjures up a colourful image in words and music. The song really came of age at The Band's farewell concert in 1976, a star-studded show that produced the live triple album and Martin Scorsese film *The Last Waltz* two years later, with Morrison giving it his all while a brass section punches out the riffs behind him. It comes to a climax when he starts dancing around spontaneously and saunters off the stage, leaving the musicians slightly bemused as they bring it to a rousing conclusion.

'Into the Mystic'

Like many other singer-songwriters, the ever-inscrutable Morrison was often reluctant to be drawn on the meanings of his songs, allowing journalists' and listeners' imaginations to run riot. This is probably the album's most enigmatic moment, a song he once said was 'just about being part of the universe'. The most likely theories are that it was inspired in part by his memories of younger days growing up in the port of Belfast, gazing at the waterside, perhaps dreaming of a life of adventure, mystery and exploration ahead as he can 'hear the sailors cry, smell the sea and feel the sky, let our soul and spirit fly, into the mystic'. An introspective arrangement featuring mainly acoustic guitar and piano builds gently, then a reference to hearing a distant foghorn evokes an appropriate response from a saxophone and the rhythm section gradually gathers pace.

'Come Running'
There are no such deep meanings behind the song that begins side two. A jaunty song with something of a country flavour, a shuffling beat with drums and conga, playful boogie-woogie piano and touches from saxophone, it was an obvious choice for a single and gave Morrison a minor hit in the spring.

'These Dreams of You'
A gently rolling blues rhythm sets the pace as this opens with acoustic guitar, slide guitar and harmonica, with a warm organ sound and saxophone enhancing the mood and evoking a Memphis soul feel. Lyrically, it is an enigmatic number, reportedly inspired by a dream Morrison had of an attempt on the life of Ray Charles. Another theory suggests that part of the song may be about his friend Richard Manuel of The Band, hence the opening line 'I hear you paid your dues in Canada'.

'Brand New Day'
One of the simplest songs on the album, at five minutes, it is also the longest. Country meets gospel, and this is almost hymn-like, especially with the presence of the backing vocalists. To a subtle backing of piano and steel guitar, Morrison sings of having been 'used, abused and so confused', but finding hope and consolation in a brand new day, a brighter tomorrow.

'Everyone'
This brings a celebratory mood from the start, beginning with a couple of lines on clavinet, sounding like a harpsichord, and suggesting something of a debt towards Bach; flourishes, and a break on the flute, all set to an almost marching beat. Rather like the previous number, it is 'a song of hope', as its writer himself said, a mood and feeling of making dreams come true if we want them to.

'Glad Tidings'
Anyone looking for something of the 'Brown Eyed Girl' vibe will find their quest amply fulfilled by the closing track. There is a similar sunny mood, an

uncomplicated 'la-la-la' refrain, even a similarity in the chord sequence, as it brings the album and its wishes of 'we'll send you glad tidings from New York' to a cheerful, upbeat conclusion.

Bridge Over Troubled Water – Simon and Garfunkel

Personnel:
Paul Simon: lead vocals, acoustic guitar, percussion
Art Garfunkel: lead vocals, percussion
Los Incas: Peruvian instruments
Joe Osborn: bass
Larry Knechtel: piano, organ
Fred Carter, Jr: acoustic and electric guitars
Pete Drake: pedal steel guitar, flute
Hal Blaine: drums, percussion
Jimmie Haskell, Ernie Freeman: strings
Buddy Harman: percussion
Bob Moore: double bass
Charlie McCoy: bass harmonica
Eddie Simon: guitar
Norman Rogers: trumpet
Produced at Columbia Studio B and E, New York City; CBS Columbia Square, Los Angeles; St Paul's Chapel, Columbian University; Iowa State University, Ames, Iowa ('Bye Bye Love' only), November 1968-November 1969 by Paul Simon, Art Garfunkel and Roy Halee.
UK release date: February 1970. US release date: January 1970
Record label: UK: CBS, US: Columbia
Highest chart places: UK: 1, US: 1
Running time: 36:29
All songs written by Paul Simon, unless stated otherwise.

The two members of popular music's favourite duo had been visibly growing apart. The studio album that was to become their parting shot was also their most eclectic and varied set, but with Garfunkel increasingly involved in a film career, much of the credit was due to Simon's insistence of moving into other musical genres beyond their crystalline, almost completely unadorned vocal harmonies and acoustic guitar-driven setting, something he would pursue increasingly in his solo career. Their sales had been increasing with each studio album, but *Bridge* beat the lot, the single and album topping charts worldwide.

In years to come, the duo would have further brief recording sessions and even a few more concerts together. Yet the differences between them would be irreconcilable, and no more studio albums resulted. Although some critics found it 'overblown and over-produced' at the time, the general verdict is that *Bridge* capped a career in being their best and most varied, as well as indisputably most successful record ever in terms of sales as well as artistry.

'Bridge Over Troubled Water'

Simon had always seen the title track as a gospel song, and invited keyboard player Larry Knechtel to play piano with this in mind. Initially, it consisted of only two verses. Thinking it too short, Garfunkel recommended adding a third, which Simon promptly supplied. After initial reluctance, Garfunkel agreed to sing lead vocal, once arranger Jimmie Haskell had transposed the score and lowered the pitch. The 'silver girl' of the first line in the last verse was a reference to Simon's then-wife, and so popular belief has it, her first grey hairs. The backing was planned carefully, and much of the dramatic effect comes from the delicate yet striking piano introduction, which is more or less the only instrument heard until the end of the second verse, punctuated by a neat tap on the cymbals from Blaine, and the bridge to the final verse, with subtly underpinning bass, strings, horns and above all drums recorded in an echo chamber for added effect. From the gentlest of beginnings, it culminated in a mighty finish worthy of some of the classic Phil Spector productions. Some of the musicians involved had played on sessions under the wayward genius himself. With its universal message of comfort, reassurance and optimism, it struck a deep emotional chord with many a listener. Several others have covered it, perhaps none more incongruously than Linda Clifford, whose disco version was a hit in 1979.

'El Condor Pasa (If I Could)' (Daniel Alomia Robles, arranged by Jorge Milchberg, English lyrics by Paul Simon)

Simon's experiments with world music, something Western musicians had rarely explored until then, started with a Peruvian song based on traditional Andean music, to which he wrote his own lyrics. He had assumed the tune to be in the public domain, until a lawsuit was filed by film director Armando Robles Godoy, whose father had written the melody in 1913 and duly registered his copyright. Simon's vocals, celebrating freedom ('I'd rather sail away like a swan that's here and gone') in a charmingly simple, nursery-rhyme like style, are given the lightest of instrumental accompaniment by the strings and pan pipes of Los Incas. It was the third single from the album in America (reaching number 18), while a cover version by Julie Felix had already been a British hit in the spring.

'Cecilia'

The duo were playing around with various percussion effects, like banging on items of furniture, and adding other sounds such as a falling bundle of drumsticks. Simon's brother Eddie provided a beat on a piano bench and guitarist Stu Scharf played chords, opening and then quickly dampening the strings. Everything was taped on a cassette recorder with added reverb, and they then passed the results to Halee, who devised a rhythm track with added xylophone from Simon. He made up the lyrics by singing along spontaneously about a girl who was breaking his heart, making love to him in the afternoon, and then carrying on with his friend while he got up to wash his face. There was, however, a happy ending in the last verse. It was released as a speedy follow-up single to 'Bridge' in America (reaching number four), but in Britain, it appeared about six months later, by which time so many people had bought the album that it never got beyond the Top 50 breakers.

'Keep the Customer Satisfied'

This made two songs in a row that were uncharacteristically poppy for the duo, as well as the third with minimal vocal involvement from Garfunkel. Yet there was a darker side to the lyric, born of Simon's frustration as a performer, laying bare his weariness of having to please audiences night after night on gruelling tours. Those who did not pay too much attention to the words could not but revel in a joyous tune with irresistible singalong chorus and full-tilt brass section. It would have made a surefire single hit had it not been on the B-side of 'Bridge'.

'So Long, Frank Lloyd Wright'

A tribute to the famous architect was also partly a song for Garfunkel, who had previously studied architecture. It had a subtext in that Simon was also subtly calling his musical partner Frank Lloyd Wright, recalling the nights they would harmonise until dawn and alluding to their being about to go their separate ways. Halee even calls out 'So long, Artie!' during the fadeout. Garfunkel later commented on his annoyance about not having been let in on the secret himself when they recorded it, although he admitted it was a beautiful song. Accompanying their harmonies was Simon's guitar, played in a Latin jazz style with plenty of seventh chords – he had been listening to Brazilian music before writing the melody – plus congas, strings, bass and flute.

'The Boxer'

Side two begins with the song that preceded the album by nearly a year as a worldwide top-ten single (top ten in the UK and the USA), at over five minutes the longest track. In this almost autobiographical lyric, Simon compares himself to a fighter, going down after one blow after another, 'but the fighter still remains'. There are references to him seeking not fame and fortune, but workman's wages, instead only getting a come-on from 'the whores on seventh avenue' – quite a racy subject for pop music in the 1960s. It was recorded in several different locations over about 100 hours studio time (and even a chapel for one section), with special attention to the drums, recorded in a corridor to produce the required echo, on the 'lie-la-lie' refrain, plus pedal steel guitar, piccolo flute strings, horns and bass harmonica. Bob Dylan loved the song so much that he recorded a (markedly inferior) version on his next album, *Self Portrait*.

'Baby Driver'

The B-side to the foregoing track was another commercial number that was anything but folk. Musically, it resembled The Beach Boys more than anyone else, with its up-tempo story of a well-brought-up boy with a comfortable life who cannot wait for his girlfriend to make him a man, far removed from his over-protected existence. Twanging guitars, a belting saxophone and car engine sound effects all contribute to one of the album's most instant numbers.

'The Only Living Boy in New York'
The duo's harmonies are particularly beguiling on this song, with a section of multi-tracked 'aaah's, the sound enhanced through being recorded like the drums in an echo chamber, a softer version of Spector's wall of sound. Yet the subject is a sombre one. It was written while Garfunkel was filming in Mexico, and Simon was in NYC, writing songs and longing for them to resume work on recording together. It opens and closes with gently strummed and picked acoustic guitar, with bass and washes of Knechtel's organ throughout much of the rest.

'Why Don't You Write Me'
At a time when reggae had yet to achieve respectability among the more hip rock music fraternity, Simon was eager to embrace the genre and would do so regularly during his later solo career. Here was his first experiment at celebrating the style that had given Jimmy Cliff and Johnny Nash their first taste of chart success. A pulsating rhythm section, forceful lead guitar, horns and a few falsetto vocal harmonies all add colour to the tale of a man stuck in the jungle and longing to hear from his other half.

'Bye Bye Love' (Felice and Boudleaux Bryant)
The only cover version on the album is a live version of the 1957 Everly Brothers' hit. One slight difference between the two duos is that Simon and Garfunkel do not add a pause in the chorus between the two 'byes'. There is evidently a band behind them, with lead guitar and drums – possibly overdubbed afterwards – but they are much less prominent in the recording than the audience, who clap along energetically throughout.

'Song for the Asking'
The applause after the last chord of the previous track segues into a closing farewell, at less than two minutes long, the shortest number. Backed by only acoustic guitar and strings, Simon sings of being 'more than glad to change [his] ways for the asking'. It could be interpreted as a desire to perform for anyone who wants to listen, or alternatively an invitation to his departing collaborator to return any time.

Sweet Baby James – James Taylor

Personnel:
James Taylor: guitar, vocals
Danny Kortchmar: guitar
Red Rhodes: steel guitar
John London, Randy Meisner: bass
Bobby West: double bass
Chris Darrow: fiddle
Carole King: piano, backing vocals
Russ Kunkel: drums
(Uncredited musicians: horns)
Produced at Sunset Sound, Los Angeles, December 1969, by Peter Asher.
UK release date: March 1970. US release date: February 1970
Record label: Warner Bros
Highest chart places: UK: 6, US: 3
Running time: 31:43
All songs written by James Taylor, unless stated otherwise.

Peter Asher had been James Taylor's manager and producer since his debut album in Britain, and after helping sign him to Warner Bros, on returning to America, he recruited the session musicians for this second album, seeking sympathetic players who would fit in well with, and complement the stripped-down acoustic style. As they were working on such a limited budget, it had to be completed fast. Taylor was recovering from injuries after a motorcycle accident, and had adequate time to prepare the songs. Once he was fit enough to enter the studio, they recorded two or three songs a day, with very little work needed once the basic tracks were laid down. Most were recorded quickly with the minimum of overdubs afterwards.

It received generally favourable reviews on release, although the general consensus was that it would be 'a must for folk-blues buffs' but unlikely to reach beyond a small cult following. Within weeks he had embarked on a major American tour, sales were rocketing, and he was being hailed as one of the most important new solo performers of the year.

On balance, most of the songs strike a balance between what one reviewer has called 'confessional darkness and soothing escapism'. As sales suggested, the simplicity of the record struck a chord in thousands of listeners the world over, as if they all had an inner James Taylor. The confessional mood, that of an earnest wounded soul who has been through bad experiences, sought solace in dubious substances and come out the other side, refuses to wallow in self-pity and still looks for a brighter day, helped to set the template for a 1970s school of singer-songwriters on both sides of the Atlantic.

'Sweet Baby James'

The title song is not autobiographical, but a waltz in 3/4 time to his little nephew, the son of his elder brother Alex. On returning to America, James learned that Alex had become a father for the first time in his absence, with a baby son, named James, after his uncle. He wrote it while on his way to Richmond, Virginia, to see the family, having been inspired by the old nursery rhyme 'Rock-a-bye baby', and adapting it to 'Rock-a-bye, sweet baby James'. The song 'just assembled itself as he was driving down there,' he recalled, and he wrote it down as soon as he returned home afterwards. It is part lullaby, part the story of a young cowboy spending lonely nights in the canyons, with no company except his horse and his cattle, as he spends the hours of darkness singing himself to sleep. Like several of the other songs, the main instrument is his acoustic guitar, with basically just the rhythm section plus wistful steel guitar, and a discreet touch on the piano, and the result is charming without descending into tweeness. It was released as the first single in America, but failed to chart.

'Lo and Behold'
With its gospel flavour, this calls to mind the spirituals that the family doubtless heard and grew up with, shot through with references to 'don't build no heathen temples' and how 'everyone's talking 'bout the train to glory', providing a hint of religious satire. The only percussion is Taylor gently tapping his foot in time to the music (it is a measure of the relaxed attitude to his music that nobody decided to re-record it but left it as it was) behind his guitar picking, and some multi-tracking on the vocals for the chorus.

'Sunny Skies'
Taylor wrote this during his treatment at the Austen Riggs Center, a psychiatric treatment facility in Stockbridge, Massachusetts. The tune is relatively cheerful, which is ironic given the sadness of the lyrics, as the title does not refer to a bright day, but a friendless character who sleeps in the morning, weeps in the evening, and does not know when to rise as he is so depressed. In the last verse, the character telling the story sings of looking out of the window at snow and trees, musing on whether he should just let the world pass him by. Taylor said that 'Sunny Skies' was the stage name for a Pakistani R'n'B singer, but he modelled it on the character of a man whom he had befriended. He added the line about 'You'll be pleased to find he ain't got no friends', as a 'rude turnaround', as the song had been 'too rosy up to that point'. Musically it follows a sprightly, soft shuffle-jazz tempo, although the only instrumentation is his finger-picked guitar.

'Steamroller Blues'
If the album seems a shade too serious up to that point, Taylor then cuts loose. Here is a bit of fun, a good-natured piece of mockery of the pretentiousness of white blues bands trying to be super-hip. With lines about being 'a cement mixer for you baby, a churnin' urn of burnin' funk', about promising to 'inject your soul, with some sweet rock'n'roll, and shoot you full of rhythm'n'blues', or being 'a napalm bomb for you baby, guaranteed to blow your mind', there

was no danger of anyone taking this seriously. Swaggering horns add a bold touch from the end of the second verse onwards. Taylor was delighted when Elvis Presley performed the song regularly on stage and had a number 17 hit with it in 1973, though it was relegated to a B-side in Britain.

'Country Road'

The previous track's mood of letting go continues. Fired up by rather more prominent drums than usual as well as piano and bass, it was inspired by Taylor's period of self-referral to McLean Hospital, Belmont, Massachusetts five years earlier, and looking to a life in which he can take to the highway. There is also a hint of defiance of parental authority; his mother fails to understand, wants to know where he's been and he would 'have to be some kind of natural-born fool to want to pass that way again'. A slightly re-recorded version was recorded at the end of the year and became a Top 40 American hit, the album's second charting single.

'Oh, Susannah' (Stephen Foster)

The album's only non-original number dates from the mid-19th century. Long since part of the American folksong heritage, it was one of those songs which would have been part of the Taylors' childhood, and here he plays it straight with acoustic guitar and no embellishments. Rather unexceptional, it is arguably no more than filler.

'Fire and Rain'

Side two opens with the song that helped make Taylor a household name. In three verses, this harrowingly autobiographical number encapsulates several elements of his life story up to the age of twenty when he wrote it. The lyrics lay bare his reactions to the death of Suzanne, an old flame, who died from a drugs overdose after being put in an isolation cell (he was not told for some time, as nobody wanted to distract him from his burgeoning musical career), his arrival in England when first trying for the big time, and a five-month period of recuperation at Austin Riggs, a rehabilitation centre at Stockbridge, Massachusetts. The on-off battles with depression and drug addiction are referenced, as are 'sweet dreams and Flying Machines', the latter being an early band formed with long-time friend Danny Kortchmar, 'in pieces on the ground'. Taylor and Asher worked hard to create the right ambience for this song with the other musicians, suggesting Kunkel use brushes instead of sticks on his drum kit, and getting West to play an upright bowed bass (sometimes mistaken for viola or cello) to produce a drone sound on the bottom note. It was chosen as the second single while Taylor was touring, and he was surprised that such a personal number proved so appealing to audiences, reaching number three in America and the Top 50 in Britain. Within a few years, it had been covered by several other artists, including John Denver, Willie Nelson, Georgie Fame, and The Isley Brothers.

'Blossom'

This lightens the mood considerably. There are no hidden meanings to the charming pastoral song of a weary soul seeking solace at the end of a long day and something to 'melt my cares away', with a light touch on acoustic guitar and a gentle pattern on the drums.

'Anywhere Like Heaven'

Another sweet ballad driven by steel guitar, in similar vein to the proceeding song, this conveys a mood of yearning for freedom and 'a pasture in the countryside'.

'Oh Baby, Don't You Loose Your Lip on Me'

Taylor could not resist a brief return to the blues. He and Kortchmar improvised it in the studio one night between them, fooling around on acoustic guitars and whatever nonsense lines came into the former's head – 'don't you loose your lovin' lip on poor old man JT'. The introductory off-the-cuff laughter is left in at the start, and Kortchmar thought it was such a throwaway that he was startled to find it on the completed album.

'Suite for 20G'

Perhaps there was a shortage of songs towards the end. Taylor and Asher were one short (although at just over half an hour, the album is hardly long), and instead of Taylor sitting down to write one more to order, they assembled one from fragments from three old compositions. Almost at once, it sounds like a collective effort with rhythm section and horns gently punctuating the verses, until about halfway through when they all let rip. Although lasting under five minutes, this evokes memories of The Beatles' segue that concluded side two of *Abbey Road*, as horns, guitar and drums settle on a steady groove to the final fadeout. The title refers to the album's creators receiving a $20,000 bonus on completing their efforts.

Déjà Vu – Crosby, Stills, Nash & Young

Personnel:
David Crosby: guitars, vocals
Stephen Stills: guitars, keyboards, bass, vocals
Graham Nash: guitars, keyboards, vocals
Neil Young: guitars, keyboards, harmonica, vocals
Greg Reeves: bass
Dallas Taylor: drums
Jerry Garcia: pedal steel guitar
John Sebastian: harmonica
Produced at Wally Heider's Studios, San Francisco and Los Angeles, July-December
1969 by Crosby, Stills, Nash & Young.
UK release date: May 1970. US release date: March 1970
Record label: Atlantic
Highest chart places: UK: 5, US: 1
Running time: 36:24

While Britain's favourite musical quartet were splintering, across the Atlantic
another somewhat fractious quartet were joining forces. Rather like The
Beatles in their later years together, Crosby, Stills, Nash and Young were
four individuals who tended to record their own songs more or less solo,
sometimes overdubbing most of the instruments themselves, and using
the others as session musicians to provide whatever else was needed.
Coincidentally, in 1968, Crosby, Stills and Nash, as a trio, had briefly based
themselves in London, where Peter Asher and George Harrison both listened
to some of their music but decided against signing them to Apple, as well as
Taylor. Later they added Neil Young, like Stills, a onetime member of Buffalo
Springfield. Sessions took about 800 hours of studio time, and Stills said that
completing *Déjà Vu* 'was like pulling teeth'. Yet it demonstrated that once a
group of sparring, strong-minded talents, all equally important, could put
their differences aside long enough, the final product could be something
really special.

Though the harmonies are tight, they did not collaborate closely on several
of the songs while recording. Apart from 'Woodstock', they were initially laid
down as individual sessions by each member, with the others later making
their contributions as required. Young appears on only half of the tracks, and
generally recorded his own songs alone in Los Angeles, brought them to the
recording studio so they could add their voices as required, then took them
away to mix himself. Some of them included more members than others,
although their recollections are sometimes conflicting. According to Young,
in an interview five years later, the band sessions were 'Helpless', 'Woodstock'
and 'Almost Cut My Hair'. The others were combinations by some but not
all, recorded by one person using the other people. Taylor and Reeves
played on most tracks, while Jerry Garcia and John Sebastian guested on one

apiece. Rumour suggests that an uncredited Nicky Hopkins also contributed occasional piano.

This would always be the most successful album in which any of them were involved, collectively and individually. Within months they had disbanded, and there would be partial and full reunions plus tours, with successful studio and live records resulting, but they would never reach this pinnacle again.

'Carry On' (Stills)

The opening track, a predominantly acoustic and upbeat country-rock tune, is coloured by vocal harmonies from all four and sprightly yet powerful lead guitar. Recycling a few of the lines from 'Questions', a song Stills had written and recorded while a member of Buffalo Springfield, it refers to his breaking up with Judy Collins, with whom he had been romantically and professionally involved not long before. Although the lyrics are suffused with sadness and regret, there is an optimistic tone as befits the title, with its message of 'a new day, a new way, and new eyes to see the dawn'.

'Teach Your Children' (Nash)

The second of three singles from the album issued in America (rising to number 16) is the first of Nash's two contributions, a gentle country-style song with Jerry Garcia's distinctive pedal steel, and again beguiling vocal harmonies. Inspired by the relationship with his father, who died when Nash was in his teens, its message is a plea for love and understanding between parents and their children. He had intended recording it with an English medieval folk flavour, until Stills suggested it would work better in country style.

'Almost Cut My Hair' (Crosby)

From one of the album's sweetest songs to the most abrasive, this song about hippies versus the establishment recalls John Lennon at his harshest. He insisted that they all cut it live in the studio with the minimum of overdubs. Although in a dark place during sessions for the album and sometimes barely able to work because of substance abuse and grief at the recent death of his girlfriend in a car crash, he insisted on turning up as scheduled. He almost spits the words out in fury – 'it increases my paranoia, like looking into a mirror and seeing a police car'. There are no vocal harmonies to sweeten the pill, and Nash's organ sounds almost as jagged as Young's guitar work. On an album of what is by and large relatively polished material, this stands out as the most direct and in-your-face four minutes.

'Helpless' (Young)

Young's soothing first contribution could hardly come as more of a contrast. His high-pitched, almost frail vocal, and Stills' country-style steel guitar complement the three-chord-based swaying tune, as he reminiscences on his old Ontario home. The rich tapestry of harmony vocals on the chorus is a delight, but most of the instruments, including acoustic and electric guitars, keyboards and harmonica, were Young's work. A song he had first recorded in Canada with his 'other' band Crazy Horse the previous year, it would become one of his signature tunes as a solo performer on stage.

'Woodstock' (Mitchell)

Following one song written by each member, side one closes with the only non-original. Joni Mitchell did not play at the festival in 1969 but wrote a song about it later that year, largely based on Nash's accounts of being there, and their versions are very different. Stills had arranged and recorded it with another band the previous September, taking lead vocals while Jimi Hendrix played bass and later overdubbed guitar, their collaboration appearing in 2018 on the Hendrix compilation *Both Sides of the Sky*. Here, as an engineer said, the result is more like 'Crosby, Stills and Hendrix' – an almost brutally rocking four minutes taken at lively pace, with some tweaks to the melody and chord sequence, especially in the chorus. It remains the best-known version in America, as the most successful of three singles from the album (reaching number 11). Stills contributes a muscular guitar riff and colourful organ as well as lead vocal, although as ever the others' harmonies provide a touch of colour to complement the rough edges. According to Young, they originally recorded it with all four singing and playing on the same session, and it 'was magic'. Later they argued that the vocal was out of tune, so Stills erased his track and added another, apparently inferior one.

'Déjà Vu' (Crosby)

The title track is probably the most free-form of all, with its shifting time signatures. A false start followed by a count-in is followed by a lazy, slightly shuffling number without any fixed rhythm, driven mostly by acoustic guitars, with choir-like backing vocals, a touch of lead guitar and John Sebastian on harmonica. The lyrics were inspired by Crosby's belief in reincarnation; the Buddhists, he said, 'have got it right – it's a wheel and we get on and get off'.

'Our House' (Nash)

Music was never less rock'n'roll than this. The third single (reaching number 30 in the US), this whimsical paean to domestic bliss, might have been subtitled 'A day in the life chez Nash and Mitchell'. While living together in Los Angeles, one morning they went out to breakfast; on the way home, they passed an antique store where she saw a vase, and immediately purchased it. As they walked through their front door, he suggested she put some flowers in it while he lit the fire. Inspiration immediately struck as he went to the piano. Within an hour he had completed the song, with references to the flowers, the vase, and their two cats in the yard. There are no guitar breaks, no guitars even, just the rhythm section behind piano, harpsichord, Nash's vocal and Crosby and Stills' harmonies – a charming song that stops just short of mawkishness. Nash soon tired of it, and despite its success as a single it only appeared on one of their five subsequent live albums, although he also played it solo in a concert at Los Angeles in November 2018 to celebrate Mitchell's 75th birthday.

'4 + 20' (Stills)

From one track performed largely solo to another completely by one individual, this describes the inner torments and reflections of an 84-year-old man on his past, born into a poor family and now alone, as he embraces the many-coloured beast, wearies of the torment, and longs for death. After recording it on his own in one take with acoustic guitar, Stills intended it for his forthcoming solo album, but the others begged him to include it here instead. When he asked Crosby and Nash to add vocal harmonies, they refused as it was 'too damn good, we're not touching it'.

'Country Girl' (Young)

This suite comprises parts of three songs, 'Whiskey Boot Hill', 'Down, Down, Down', both of which Young had written and recorded while with Buffalo Springfield, and the newer 'Country Girl'. (Most British and overseas pressings listed all three songs on the label, but not on the sleeve). Musically it is in 3/4 time, his mournful lyrics contrasting strongly with the others' gentler harmonies, with largely organ instrumentation providing an orchestral effect, even a Spectoresque wall of sound in places, harmonica at the fadeout, and guitars relegated to the background. Lyrically, as a whole, it is slightly disjointed. The first few verses are about a waitress, and musings on 'stars [who] sit in bars and decide what they're drinking, they drop by to die 'cause it's faster than sinking'. It was not one of his favourite contributions to the group, and he later called it 'overblown'.

'Everybody I Love You' (Stills-Young)

As the record began on a positive note, it ends in similar fashion with a lively song of love, optimism, even world peace. Stills leads on vocal with the others contributing harmonies, plus a tuneful torrent of guitars.

Benefit – Jethro Tull

Personnel:
Ian Anderson: vocals, acoustic and electric guitars, flute, balalaika, keyboards
Martin Barre: electric guitar
Glenn Cornick: bass, Hammond organ
Clive Bunker: drums, percussion
John Evan: piano, organ
Produced at Morgan Studios, London, September 1969-February 1970 by Ian
Anderson and Terry Ellis.
UK release date: April 1970, US release date: May 1970
Record label: Chrysalis (UK), Reprise (US)
Highest chart places: UK: 3, US: 11
Running time: 42:49
All songs written by Ian Anderson.

By the time of their third album, Jethro Tull had initially explored the
blues and subsequently a more jazzy direction. Now they seemed set fair
to work on a new sound, taking them further in the progressive folk-rock
direction. Moreover, months of playing large venues in America opening for
the likes of Led Zeppelin, Grand Funk Railroad and MC5 had encouraged
them to play harder and heavier on stage, something that was bound to be
repeated on the next album they recorded. Finally, Ian Anderson admitted
that increasing disenchantment with some aspects of the music industry
and subsequent cynicism were to be reflected in the lyrics that he was
writing at the time. He said the addition of John Evan on keyboards had
given them a new musical dimension, and he could now write more freely.
Guitarist Martin Barre felt it was an easier album to make, as the success of
the previous two had likewise given all the musicians more artistic liberty,
while Cornick, who left the group immediately afterwards, felt that they
had captured a more live feeling in the studio, rather than sounding like a
bunch of session musicians.

Taken as a whole, again to quote Anderson, it was a 'guitar riff' album,
with the shadow and influence of Jimi Hendrix, Jimmy Page and others
looming large. He called it 'rather dark and stark', and while it seemed
to him to cement the evolution of the band playing as a band, he felt it
lacked the variety of its more successful predecessor, 'Stand Up'. Several
tracks lack any formal song structure and, apart from 'Inside', it gave
the impression that they were no longer desperate to throw the record
company another potential top ten smash after a hat-trick of hits. It tends
to sound disjointed on the first few listens, especially as most tracks also
include some interesting if rather jarring studio effects and trickery. Yet
prog rock in 1970 was nothing if it was not attempting to break new
boundaries, and Jethro Tull had the talent and spirit of adventure to do so
just as well as their peers.

'With You There To Help Me'

This opens with a strange fanfare, a combination of frenzied flute, discordant laughing and doomy piano. After painting a picture of contrasts in the opening verse about 'sweet smelling summer nights of wine and song, dusty pavements, burning feet', Anderson sings of a longing for a home life, of 'going back to the ones that I know'. Over six minutes or so, the flute bubbles fiercely, and begins a kind of answering routine with Barre's slashing guitar, backed by acoustic guitar and gently throbbing bass, alongside a few changes in tempo from steady to waltz-time, slowing down and then speeding up.

'Nothing To Say'

Anderson now lets fly lyrically, and vents his irritation with constant touring, record company demands and false promises. A subtle riff from guitar, bass and staccato drumbeat lead into a number in which 'Every morning pressure forming all around my eyes, ceilings crash, the walls collapse, broken by the lies that your misfortune brought upon us', reiterating that just because he has a name he still has 'nothing to say'. Despite his anger, the song sounds relatively mellow, with swirling bass runs and piano throughout. The main bite comes from the forceful guitar breaks, contributing to a good but all-too-brief solo at the end.

'Alive and Well and Living In'

This has more of a hook than the two previous songs. Although nobody could ever suggest that Jethro Tull songs follow obvious well tried and tested rock'n'roll-inspired chord sequences, this is one of those that has an infectious quality of sorts, thanks to the unusual combination of interplay between Anderson's vocals, piano and flute. At times it veers on jazz with some sprightly runs up and down the piano, at other moments, it goes more into folk-rock territory, and a section near the end where the lead guitar and flute are in unison provide a neat touch.

'Son'

Although less than three minutes long and similarly careful not to outstay its welcome, 'Son' is one of those interesting numbers that dispenses with song structure altogether, built around a conversation between father and son. Vocals start almost at once alongside a striking guitar riff, everything fades out briefly about halfway through, and then it starts again more slowly with a different melody altogether. Lyrically, it alternates between stern parental advice and the smack of firm authority – 'Permission to breathe, Sir – Don't talk like that, I'm your old man' – and tongue-in-cheek humour – 'So son, you'd better apologise, and when you grow up, if you're good we will buy you a bike'. It comes to a sudden halt in mid-air (to signify one of the protagonists walking out and slamming the door, perhaps?), with the briefest of guitar solos.

'For Michael Collins, Jeffrey and Me'

This has often puzzled casual listeners. Michael Collins was not the Irish revolutionary leader killed in 1922, but the third member of the Apollo 11 crew at the time of the first moon landing in 1969, though he remained in the orbiting command module while his colleagues, Armstrong and Aldrin, walked on the moon instead. Jeffrey is Jeffrey Hammond-Hammond, a long-time friend of Anderson who would shortly join the group on bass guitar. (His double-barrelled name came about as his father's name and mother's maiden name were both identical). The theme of the song is not quite an answer to Bowie's 'Space Oddity', but more about the dilemma of a person whose efforts ultimately remain unfulfilled, and who finds himself or herself merely remaining on the sidelines as an observer. There are also references in the lyrics to L.E.M., the lunar lander or Lunar Excursion Module. Musically, the song starts off in quite a folksy way with acoustic guitar, joined by piano. Some powerful guitar soloing appears later, but there are several shifts between different time signatures, with an almost southern boogie-like chorus followed by a much more mellow verse.

'To Cry You a Song'

Side two begins with another song that, after the fade-in guitar riff, is dominated instrumentally throughout by Barre's soloing, plus a large helping of heavy echo and distortion on Anderson's voice. Part of the guitar work is played through a Leslie speaker, and it sounds like the same effect has been used occasionally on the vocals as well. The lyrics are about travelling home to London by plane, evidently after a gruelling tour, with references to 'chasing a dream inside its paper bag', and unnamed persons 'can't find what they're looking for, waving me through'. Some eagle-eyed listeners, noting also the opening lines of 'flying so high', have construed these as drug references. Anderson always maintained that he was firmly anti-drugs, and in an interview later admitted that with hindsight, it was naïve of him to use the 'flying' reference in song that way.

'A Time for Everything'

For the shortest song on the album, flute and guitar are playing in unison much of the time, as Anderson delivers a thoughtful, world-weary lyric: 'I'd been missing what time could bring, fifty years and I, filled with tears and joys I never cried.' There is one unusual sound for a few seconds about halfway through that sounds like flute, or possibly organ, emulating a whistling kettle.

'Inside'

The most immediate track of all, this was released as a single but received little exposure and failed to chart. A warm flute riff and bubbling sound from the guitar and drums go hand in hand with the cheerful song of a man who is comfortable at home with his wife, may have no money coming in, but is not bothered. He looks forward to having friends round for tea in the evening, and after that, to counting lambs, counting sheep as they fall into sleep, then awake to a new day of living.

'Play in Time'

On another relatively commercial piece, an insistent, even aggressive flute and guitar riff delivers a foot-tapping boogie, where both lead instruments again play in unison part of the time. Near the end, there is a burst of almost ear-shattering reverse tape effects and guitar feedback. The lyrics include another veiled riposte at the music business, as Anderson declares that he is talking to people in the way: 'Got to take in what I can, there is no time to do what must be done.'

'Sossity; You're a Woman'

An acoustic song completes the album. The title, as Anderson admits, is a weak pun on what he calls 'a rather prissy girl's name'. Or is the name really 'society'? Whatever, she is a strait-laced, fairly affluent or upper-class woman, with a 'Sunday paper voice'. He added that he was never really comfortable with the lyrics. Musically, acoustic guitar carries it most of the way, plus a couple of brief flute passages and a shake of the tambourine. To conclude, the guitar changes its time signature as it goes into a neat little Spanish journey with a flamenco chord or two at the very end.

Ladies of the Canyon – Joni Mitchell

Personnel:
Joni Mitchell: guitars, keyboards, vocals
Teresa Adams: cello
Paul Horn: clarinet, flute
Jim Horn: baritone saxophone
Milt Holland: percussion
Lookout Mountain United Downstairs Choir: vocal chorus
Recorded January 1970,
Composed and arranged by Joni Mitchell
Produced at A&M Studios, Los Angeles, January 1970 by Joni Mitchell.
UK release date: May 1970; US release date: April 1970
Record label: Reprise
Highest chart places: UK: 8, US: 27
Running time: 44:13

Joni Mitchell's third album was released just as she was being hailed as an important songwriter for others. Judy Collins had had a transatlantic hit with 'Both Sides Now', and Tom Rush featured 'The Circle Game' as the title track of an album two years earlier. One track was destined to become her best-known as a performer and her greatest hit by a mile.

As one of the first singer-songwriters (and the first woman) to make a lasting impression, her songs performed live and in the studio with little more than her own acoustic guitar and piano accompaniment – only the lightest touch of percussion, and no bass within earshot – immediately tagged her as a folksinger. Later she moved more into sophisticated soft rock-meets-jazz territory, towards which this album marked the first tentative steps.

'Morning Morgantown'

The music gets off to a warm beginning with a song dedicated to the city in West Virginia. A simple vocal and acoustic guitar opening are joined within a minute by piano, adding a sound like an old-fashioned music box as Mitchell paints a portrait in words of merchants rolling their awnings down, and milk trucks making their morning round, as two observers talk about finding themselves a table in the shade, sip their tea and lemonade, and watch the world go by. This is Joni Mitchell, the artist in more senses than one. She was responsible for the album sleeve design, and later became well-known for her pictures. More than any other, this song is full of little vignettes, or details, such as those that would catch the painter's eye.

'For Free'

A delicately tinkling piano is the main instrument heard throughout, underscored part of the way through by cello, and after the final verse, a short coda on piano and clarinet, the latter instrument still playing once the former has finished. Inspired by a busker in Manhattan playing 'real good, for free', she contemplates her own status as a wealthy performer who plays 'for fortunes', has a limousine and two gentlemen escorting her to concert halls, and after spending nights in hotels, goes shopping for jewellery. Seeing a street musician playing in very different circumstances makes her confront reality. Everybody else walks by as they have never seen him on television; she is the only one stopping to listen, and considers crossing the road to suggest a tune, or maybe even join in with a little harmony. Almost a short story as much as a song, it is an engaging reflection on artistry and fame, or the lack of it. David Crosby loved the song, and sang it on the Byrds' farewell album in 1973.

'Conversation'

This is also like a short story set to music. There are hints of a love triangle, in which she introduces a friend who joins her in the café for friendly comfort and conversation. He is trapped in a difficult relationship with a woman who speaks in sorry sentences and miraculous repentances, and 'only brings him out to show her friends'. At the end, he will ask sadly why he cannot leave this difficult partner. For most of the song, she accompanies herself on guitar, with double-tracked harmonies towards the end, much in the style of those by Crosby, Stills, Nash and Young, and in the last thirty seconds, the sounds are enriched firstly by flute and then saxophone.

'Ladies of the Canyon'

The storyteller returns in the title track, a portrait in four verses of three true-life characters living in the streets off Laurel Canyon Boulevard, in the Hollywood hills, alongside the mountain gorge near Sunset Strip that had become a bohemian refuge. The Laurel Canyon Sound became a byword for rural, domestic and feminine music. In the song, Trina is loosely based on artist and cartoonist Trina Robbins, who sews lace on widow's weeds, and embroiders her coat with leaves and vines. Annie, based on Cass Elliott of The Mamas and The Papas, is surrounded by cats and babies, adores baking, and welcomes all visitors. Estrella is Mitchell herself, a circus girl wrapped in gypsy shawls, with songs like tiny hammers hurled at bevelled mirrors in empty halls. The only instrument is guitar, with minor embellishments from a 'la-la-la' chorus towards the end. It was covered some twenty years later by Annie Lennox.

'Willy'

This was her response to Graham Nash's immortalising their months of domestic bliss in 'Our House', William being his second name. The song received its first public airing when she appeared on television a few days after the Woodstock festival in August 1969, performing it as part of a medley with 'For Free' and saying it was about 'my man'. Sitting at the piano, she sings sweetly of her relationship with the one who is her child and father, her joy and sorrow. It is no sickly love song, as she ponders the contrariness of a lover who would give her his heart 'but for an ancient injury' (maybe a reference to divorce from his first wife) and 'cannot hear the chapel's pealing silver bells'. Her words paint him as the more vulnerable partner of the two; he gave his heart too soon, and wants to run away and hide, while she is the eager starry-eyed optimist, feeling like she is just being born, like a shiny light breaking in a storm. 'Life used to be so hard', he mused in his song on *Déjà Vu*, and unlike her, maybe he still finds it thus.

'The Arrangement'

One year previously, Elia Kazan had adapted his autobiographical novel of the same name for the cinema, with a score by David Amram. Mitchell had been asked to write him lyrics for a song to be used in the picture, but Kazan decided not to use them, and she set them to music herself. Again with just piano for accompaniment, she delivers a bleak little ditty about, or rather to, a man who 'could have been more than a name on the door', and can still escape to a better life, while his wife keeps the keys as 'she is so pleased to be a part of the arrangement'.

'Rainy Night House'

A vague, similarly aborted cinematic connection features in another piano-backed song. It was inspired by her personal relationship with Leonard Cohen, after they first met at the Newport Folk Festival in 1967. Though it only lasted a few months, they remained friends until his death in 2016. She loved his song 'Suzanne', and there was talk of Hollywood producers asking him to score a film based on it, a project on which he asked her to help. It never came to anything, but their association together still inspired the song. According to the lyrics, she joined him one rainy night at his mother's home, fell asleep and he sat up all night watching her. Piano is augmented sparingly by a burst of multi-tracked vocals, 'the upstairs choir', which she references briefly in one verse, and a short burst of cello.

'The Priest'

This is probably the most enigmatic lyric on the album. She sings of a holy man who she meets in an airport bar and the lines are full of religious imagery, although the narrative is left unresolved. He 'took his contradictions out, and he splashed them on my brow', but what comes of their chance meeting, if anything at all, is left to the listener to judge.

'Blue Boy'

A poetical tale, this has hints of a medieval or renaissance-period setting. Accompanied by Chopin-like piano, it concerns the love between a woman who travels 'to place her flowers before his granite grace', and sometimes he will read to her, take her in his arms, but she would wake in the morning alone. It is a pretty song, but ultimately not one of the record's finest.

'Big Yellow Taxi'

One of the first hit singles to put environmental concerns to the fore was written after Mitchell had stayed in a Hawaii hotel. Waking up on the morning after her arrival, she drew back the curtains, saw the distant green mountains, then looked more closely and noticed a parking lot. This blight on paradise, she said, broke her heart. Her giggle near the end of this acoustic guitar-backed number was unintentional as the recording was meant to be a run-through. She did not know the tape was rolling, but liked the spontaneity and retained it. Despite the sombre message of 'don't it always seem to go – you don't know what you've got till it's gone', and lines asking the farmer to put away his DDT, the song has an airy, welcoming quality. Yet, she took the subject seriously, as her major role at the Camchitka concert later that year proved. The song is, in a way, like Rachel Carson's trailblazing book *Silent Spring* set to music.

'Woodstock'

The song commemorating the festival became familiar on both sides of the Atlantic that year in two very different other versions, Matthews Southern Comfort's laid-back rendering in Britain and Crosby, Stills, Nash & Young's rocking out earlier on. Joni's is closer to the former, accompanying herself on electric piano this time. It always had a deep emotional resonance for her, and she burst into tears the first time she performed it in public. Admittedly, as others pointed out, her absence from the event meant she did not have any experience of the mud or bad LSD.

'Circle Game'

This was inspired by 'Sugar Mountain', a song by Neil Young, whom she had known for some years. He was annoyed as he used to visit a favourite club regularly, until finding himself barred on reaching twenty-one. Mitchell thought that there would be quite a bleak future for them all on reaching maturity, so she wrote it as a song searching for hope in the face of lost youth. It is the only song on the album where the backing vocals are not hers, but by the Lookout Mountain United Downstairs Choir, alias Crosby, Stills and Nash. (Ironically Young, the song's godfather, was absent).

Let It Be – The Beatles

Personnel:
John Lennon: guitars, bass, vocals
Paul McCartney: guitars, bass, keyboards, percussion, vocals
George Harrison: guitars, tambura, vocals
Ringo Starr: drums, percussion
Billy Preston: keyboards
Linda McCartney: backing vocals
George Martin: Hammond organ, percussion
Produced at Apple, EMI and Twickenham Film Studios, London, January
1969-April 1970, by Phil Spector and (uncredited) George Martin.
UK and US release date: May 1970
Record label: Apple
Highest chart places: UK: 1, US: 1
Running time: 35:10
All songs credited to John Lennon and Paul McCartney, unless stated otherwise.

'This is us with our trousers off, so will you please end the game now?' John
Lennon reputedly said with regard to the release of what were originally
dubbed the 'Get Back' sessions for the last album they completed as a group
(*Abbey Road* was recorded in its entirety after this was started, but finished and
issued several months earlier). George Martin was the initial producer, but the
group put the tapes on one side and Phil Spector was later called in to complete
the job. When EMI told Martin he would not receive an official credit, he replied
it should read 'Produced by George Martin, over-produced by Phil Spector'.

All things considered, the album has its good moments. But in hindsight, it
really does not compare well with what had gone before, and is really only one
for the Fab Four completist – of whom naturally there are many. From the sound
of the record, The Beatles were enjoying themselves at times, but on some
numbers, they sound forced, their hearts not really in it, as if they have the germ
of a good idea to start with but can no longer be tempted to see it through
properly. Were they putting their instruments away afterwards with a feeling of
'OK, that'll do', before getting out of the studio as quickly as possible? Lennon's
dismissive remarks at the start of this review ring all too true.

As for Phil Spector, who had some pretty thin gruel at his disposal, he
undeniably enhanced the sound in places, and his contribution, like the
curate's egg, was excellent in parts. It might be too harsh to say that he tried
to make a silk purse out of a sow's ear, but the thought is there. The only
alternative might have been for George Martin to call them to order, but by
then, they had become an uncomfortable coalition who no longer wanted to
work together and who had nothing left to prove. Those who would prefer
a de-Spectorised version without the false starts, additional dialogue, 'Dig It'
and 'Maggie Mae' (which should both have been left on one of the group's
Christmas fan club flexidiscs), and with Lennon's 'Don't Let Me Down', the

B-side of 'Get Back', added, would be advised to seek out the 2003 alternative *Let It Be…Naked* as well – or instead.

'Two of Us'

Introduced by a few seconds of Lennon banter, this is plainly a McCartney song, very much in line with the style he would follow throughout much of his solo career, a homely unassuming lyric of friendship on which they share vocals. A further touch of warmth comes with a little whistled quote at the end from 'Hello Goodbye'.

'Dig a Pony'

Clearly Lennon's song, after a fluffed start (followed by the sound of someone blowing his nose), it becomes a slow-paced, almost waltz-like, bluesy tune. There is nothing to the lyrics, a series of ad-libbed disconnected phrases, but it is redeemed a little by the vocal harmonies, some hard-rocking guitar, and Starr's drumming well up in the mix. Its creator later dismissed it, not surprisingly, as 'garbage'.

'Across the Universe'

This reveals the softer side of Lennon. First recorded in 1968, it was considered as a single until the group came up with 'Lady Madonna', then given as an exclusive to *No One's Gonna Change Our World*, a World Wildlife Fund charity album the following year. It was subsequently remixed by Spector, who removed the wildlife sound effects and backing vocals provided by two teenage fans who had been hanging around outside and were invited into the studio, and added vocal and string overdubs. A pleasant, dreamy song of an ideal world, it was one its creator later called one of his best, though he was dissatisfied with the final result, saying the vocals and guitars were out of tune.

'I Me Mine'

This went down in history as the last song on which the Beatles (make that the Lennon-less Threetles) ever worked together in the studio, at least until the 1990s and the two Lennon demos reworked for the first two *Anthology* compilations. Originally only 90 seconds long, it was expanded by Spector's splicing the tape to repeat the chorus and one of the verses. Lyrically, it is slight and very repetitive, with a vague message about the selfishness of humanity – maybe directed at the other Beatles (or two of them, at any rate) – but the variations in tempo, part waltz, part rocker, and the overdubbed choir, strings and brass help to make a difference for the better.

'Dig It'

While arguably the least necessary track on the record, it is, fortunately, less than a minute long. It was culled from a twelve-minute improvised jam, with

Lennon saying whatever comes into his head (mostly 'Like a rolling stone' several times), finishing off by introducing in a high-pitched voice, 'Hark the herald angels come'. It was clearly a dig at what follows – very amusing, John, but schoolboy jokes like this are only funny once and then become tiresome. Time to stop.

'Let It Be'

This song was the butt of Lennon's humour. McCartney's title track had been a single two months before the album. Here, Spector has remixed Martin's original production, most evident in a different and more forceful guitar solo taken from a much later session, some enhancement to the drums, and additional strings.

'Maggie Mae'

More filler, with Lennon leading the others in a minute's worth from an old Liverpudlian folk song. The uncharitable thought occurs that Lennon, having long regarded himself as the senior member of the group, and resenting the fact that McCartney had been gradually taking over leadership from around the time of the *Sergeant Pepper* sessions onwards, is showing off as the naughty boy in class who hardly cares if he gets expelled by the headmaster as long as he can have his fun first.

'I Got a Feeling'

This was basically a suite comprising McCartney's incomplete song of the same title and Lennon's similarly unfinished 'Everybody Had a Hard Year'. Some hard-rocking guitar, screamed vocals, and Preston's electric piano are the song's good points, but overall the effect is of a mishmash cobbled together out of necessity. It was, however, the last both men delivered as an active writing partnership.

'One After 909'

After the last Lennon-McCartney collaboration, the album jumps to one of the earliest. In his late teens, Lennon attempted to write 'a bluesy freight train-type song'. With some McCartney tweaks, they first recorded it in 1963 but felt it could be improved. Six years later they revived it, and again with Preston's electric piano, it comes across as a lively good-time rocker that was fun to play, and obviously would not have sounded out of place on one of the first albums. A couple of takes from the original session appeared in 1994 on *Anthology 1*.

'The Long and Winding Road'

This became famous as the McCartney song which was one of the straws that broke the camel's back. He had been inspired to write it by the landscape around his farm in the Highlands, and the group recorded it early in the sessions, again with Preston as well as McCartney on keys. Over a year later, Spector Mantovani-ised it with harps, horns and a female choir. It infuriated the song's creator, who said angrily in an interview that he would never have female voices on a Beatles record, forgetting his wife Linda had contributed backing vocals to the album's title track. The song still has a certain grandeur and is one of the few relatively polished numbers on the album, but it is easy to see why he thought it had been over-sweetened and trivialised.

'For You Blue'

On one of the few playful numbers that really works, Harrison picks acoustic guitar and croons his way through an infectious twelve-bar blues song, written for his wife Pattie, ad-libbing references to Elmore James and 'Go Johnny Go' while Lennon plays slide on a lap steel guitar. It is one of the most fun on the album, though not the greatest song to start with. Was Harrison frustrated at his compositions being regarded as lightweight, and therefore tossing the group the crumbs from his table while stockpiling the better quality work for his own solo career? And as a very proficient slide guitar player himself, did he not find it ironic that he was not playing it on his own song – or merely not bothered, resigned to the fact that the Beatle days were now numbered?

'Get Back'

Already familiar as a chart-topper the previous spring, the track after which the album was initially named closes it. This is the same take as the single, although altered slightly by Spector to make buyers think they were getting a different recording. He added some studio banter at the start, removed the start-again and fade-out coda with which the single had ended, and substituted Lennon's off-the-cuff remarks from the Apple Office rooftop session in which he thanked the audience and told them he hoped they had passed the audition.

Live at Leeds – The Who

Personnel:
Roger Daltrey: lead vocals, harmonica
Pete Townshend: guitar, backing vocals
John Entwistle: bass, backing vocals
Keith Moon: drums, backing vocals
Recorded on 14 February 1970, University of Leeds Refectory, remixed and
produced by Jon Astley, Kit Lambert, and The Who at Townshend's home studio.
UK and US release date: May 1970
Record label: Track
Highest chart places: UK: 3 US: 4
Running time: 37:42

After returning from an American tour in late 1969, The Who had decided
that releasing a live album comprising material recorded at the concerts was a
priority for them. One reason was that they knew they could not bottle all the
sound and the fury that they unleashed in front of an eager audience on a good
night onto a long-player lovingly crafted in a state-of-the-art studio behind
closed doors, and the other was that it would pay to beat the bootleggers at
their own game. The sleeve design, with its rubber-stamp design for the title,
was a deliberate attempt to mimic the style of the vinyl pirates.

On reflection, they realised that having to sift through 80 hours of tapes
and choose the best from them was not a task to be approached lightly, if at
all. Rumour has it that in a moment of madness, the tapes were thrown on a
bonfire. Instead, they scheduled two gigs in England, one at Hull and one at
Leeds University, which between them would provide all they needed. There
were technical issues with the sound quality from both recordings, notably a
faulty microphone cable, but the latter proved superior. A warning statement,
'Crackling Noises OK – Do Not Correct', appeared on the record label.

They were keen for it to be released as soon as possible. Some vocal
overdubs and minor editing were required, but the work was done quickly and
it reached the shops three months later. From a repertoire of over 30 songs
performed on stage, including 20 from 'Tommy' in the middle, just six were
chosen. Subsequent reissues have made more tracks available on CD (a single,
a double, and even a quadruple boxed set), and more recently, the complete
gig digitally.

On this original six-track helping, the first two songs you hear were numbers
five and six respectively, on the full setlist that night. The other four came right
at the end, following a generous selection of excerpts from 'Tommy'. As far as
the vinyl version goes, side one contains the shorter tracks, all less than five
minutes long.

Throughout the performances, all four members let rip and throw finesse
to the winds. In particular, Moon really tests his drum kit to the limits, and
you can almost see the sweat roll off him as he punishes the cymbals in all

directions. The limitations of vinyl not only precluded the addition of further numbers (although side one clocks in at a less than generous fifteen minutes, suggesting room for at least one more) but also put paid to sneaking in any on-stage announcements, something that would have enhanced the atmosphere a little more.

Nevertheless, in its original form, it remains an excellent document, or at least a generous taster of what they sounded like on stage, and gave them a chance to play three thoroughly reworked cover versions of old standards. Over the years, it has regularly topped 'best live album of all time' polls.

'Young Man Blues' (Mose Allison)

This had been regularly in their stage show since 1964 when they were still The High Numbers. Here it is a masterful howl of rage, a song that carries a similar message to 'My Generation', as Daltrey proclaims that 'a young man ain't got nothin' in the world these days', and proves himself a match for Robert Plant in the screaming stakes. There are plenty of stop-start sections, with guitar and rhythm section alternately pushing the decibels to their limit one moment and cutting out for the vocals, and an instrumental jam midway through.

'Substitute' (Townshend)

While the album is anything but a 'greatest hits live', a crisp version of their 1966 top-five entry comes next. Always a stage favourite, its impact this time is slightly reduced by the fact that they race through it rather hurriedly, bringing it to an end after the choruses that follow the second verse, dispensing altogether with the break and repeated third verse plus choruses. It clocks in at just over two minutes, a good ninety seconds shorter than the original single. That apart there are no complaints, with the only-just-noticeable backing vocal lines still intact.

'Summertime Blues' (Jerry Capehart, Eddie Cochran)

The first of two rock'n'roll standards that inspired so many a group of the time, Cochran's original is secure in everyone's affections, but The Who follow San Francisco power trio Blue Cheer in seizing it by the scruff of the neck and extracting every ounce of teenage rebellion from the lyrics that they can. Daltrey sounds like he is seething with fury. At the risk of blasphemy, and no disrespect intended, they make Cochran's original version sound tame by comparison. This is sheer anger with its larger-than-life powerful chords, a blistering solo from Townshend, and the authority call and response lines ('I'd like to help you son', etc.) from Entwistle, making this the definitive version of the song. There is also a key change at the end of the break before the last verse, and in trying to hit the highest notes, Daltrey is slightly flat in places, but all credit to them for having the honesty to leave such glitches in. They had recorded the song twice in the studio three years before, the second time for a BBC Radio 1 session, but neither was released for a long time. This live version from Leeds also came out as a single.

'Shakin' All Over' (Johnny Kidd)

Johnny Kidd's anthem has long been recognised as one of the first genuine homegrown British rock'n'roll songs. On this loud and lovely outing, the chorus line is slowed down slightly to good effect, stretching the syllables on 'over'. A few extra notes embellish the opening guitar riff, and after the second verse and chorus, Moon's frenetic work on the drums, that threatens to demolish his kit altogether, leads guitarist and bassist into a frantic jam that extends to two minutes plus, about half the song, before they reprise the chorus. The original version as played on stage comprised a snatch of the riff from Willie Dixon's 'Spoonful', doubtless as a nod to its popularisation by Cream, but was edited out for copyright reasons.

'My Generation'

Two more old Who hits take a bow, but faithful copies of the singles they are not. 'My Generation' is extended to almost a quarter of an hour, but after the first two minutes of stuttering frustration, it changes direction, becoming in part a medley incorporating extracts from 'See Me, Feel Me' and quotes from other songs in 'Tommy', plus a few riffs from their then-forthcoming single 'The Seeker', and Townshend songs such as 'Naked Eye' and 'Don't Even Know Myself'. Of light and shade, even more stop-start, between the three musicians, there is plenty along the way, before the splendidly bombastic big finish.

'Magic Bus'

Almost eight minutes' worth (which for technical reasons had to be edited down from over ten) of The Who's semi-forgotten and poorly-charting single from 1968 close the show. Written about two years earlier, this was ostensibly about a vehicle that a man wanted to buy so he could visit his girlfriend every day. (Some people thought 'a magic bus' was a euphemism for something else musicians might use to take a trip). From the percussion intro with the audience clapping along in time and the Bo Diddley-like rhythm through to the jamming break that begins about three minutes in with Daltrey's seething harmonica joining in, the crescendo of drums and bursts of guitar feedback gradually leads to the dynamic end. Townshend admitted that the tape had to be edited a little as they went out of sync, but it is such an energetic performance that one needs the sharpest of ears to detect anything amiss.

Cricklewood Green – Ten Years After

Personnel:
Alvin Lee: guitar, vocals
Leo Lyons: bass
Chick Churchill: keyboards
Ric Lee: drums
Produced at Olympic Studio 1, London, by Alvin Lee, 1969.
UK and US release date: April 1970
Record label: Deram
Highest chart places: UK: 4, US: 14
Running time: 39:03

If Led Zeppelin were the undisputed masters of British blues meets hard rock with a few surprises thrown in, for a year or two TYA ran them a close second. And if Fleetwood Mac had laid down the template for the blues with the imagination to break the mould and take their music into different directions, TYA ran with the ball even further. Still basking in the aftermath of their stateside success at the Newport, Seattle, and above all Woodstock festivals in the summer of 1969, shortly before they returned to Britain and entered the studio again, they were clearly at their peak, and this fourth studio album was indisputably their greatest moment. Frontman Alvin Lee had a reputation as the fastest guitarist in town. While meaningful lyrics may never have been his strongest calling card, one having the impression that most if not all of their songs were improvised in the studio, his relentless battery of guitar riffs and the ability to write songs in various other genres such as folk, jazz and country provided ample compensation.

TYA's reign as one of the top groups in their field was brief. While the potential to develop their music was there, they never really lived up to the promise of this album, their most successful outing, and they seem less remembered fifty years on than they deserve. In their love of riff-driven blues-rock, they were not a million miles away from the likes of Zeppelin, Canned Heat or even turn-of-the-decade Status Quo. However, they did not have the same ear as the latter for an infectious boogie, or a second vocalist to alternate with Lee or provide vocal harmonies, something that would have given them more of a commercial edge and another hit single or two – or at least a co-producer who could have nudged them in a direction that might have meant greater longevity. Yet on this album, they were assured of their fifteen minutes of fame in the first division.

'Sugar the Road'
Ushered in by a few seconds of synthesiser bloops and whooshes, as if aliens have arrived on planet earth from outer space, a steady drumbeat then arrives to kick the first track into an eager groove with guitar, organ and bass all fiercely cooking. There are almost shades of 'Born To Be Wild' in the sheer attack of instrumental sounds, although Alvin Lee's vocals are gruffer. The

71

guitar solo mounts a full-frontal assault, with Ric Lee's sterling work on the drums and especially upfront work on the cymbals to match.

'Working on the Road'

More variations on the theme enter here. On one level, the riffs are almost mind-numbingly simple, but there is an infectious quality in the way they are played that means the notes stay firmly in your head after a few listens. So, for those with sharp ears, does a small *faux pas* just under a minute in, where someone leant on the faders during recording or mixing just long enough to interrupt the flow for a split second. Warts and all, they decided to leave it in.

'50,000 Miles Beneath My Brain'

The album's longest track at just over seven and a half minutes takes it all to new heights. A deceptively laid-back intro demonstrates well their ability to develop their ideas from gentle beginnings, not least with some nifty touches from Churchill on harpsichord. Two minutes in, Lee is singing himself into a sweat as the main three-chord riff gathers pace, ad-libbing vocals throughout the jamming that follows, with a positive storm on his guitar soloing into the fadeout and brief fade-in again. Like many a track of similar length, it ebbs and flows throughout, and sometimes sounds as if almost in danger of falling off the rails, but then just as quickly, it gets back on track once more.

'Year 3000 Blues'

After three helpings of blues and jamming workouts, the space alien sound effects return before something completely different – a burst of sharp acoustic guitar picking straight out of Nashville. If Lee was not wearing a cowboy hat here while showing off his best Grand Ole Opry twang, then he should have been. He even offers a hint of science fiction in the lyrics, with a vision of a dystopian world in centuries to come. Our hero has been taken to the grading station, and is told that because of over-population, he will soon be dead, but he escapes from the force field and so on. The story does not develop any further than that, but it provides a gentle hint of humour or silliness, depending on your view. Clocking in at only just over two minutes, one feels that in contrast to some of the other tracks, this is one song that could have been developed a little further.

'Me and My Baby'

Here come TYA the Jazzers, as Lee and the group go boldly into Georgie Fame or Dave Brubeck territory, and this is as close as you can get to the genre without having a full-blown brass section helping out as well. Guitar solos, Hammond organ, and piano all take the spotlight in turn, to say nothing of Leo Lyons's walking bassline and drum fills.

'Love Like a Man'

A ghostly organ shimmers at first while the guitar gets into gear on one of those inimitable riffs that many aspiring teenage guitarists of the time would cut their teeth (or fingers) on. During the verses in the first two minutes, there is plenty of light and shade, almost dying away one moment and then bouncing back with fury seconds later. In the lengthy jamming section, it alternates between the basic riff and the same note, before returning for a final verse, chorus and blazing guitar solo until fading. The seven-minute album track was edited down to three minutes for a single on the A-side, making it a double-speed single with a live eight-minute version on the flip playing at 33 r.p.m., and a transatlantic chart entry. To this day, it inevitably remains their best-known number.

'Circles'

A sombre folksy song takes the stage, mostly acoustic guitar-led, with a suitably restrained organ and rhythm section. Vocals apart, this could almost be a Simon and Garfunkel number, as Lee ponders how his life is going around in circles, will it ever end, and if he dies, would he be missed at all. Like the previous out-of-character songs, it is kept fairly short, with no opportunity for extended soloing.

'As the Sun Still Burns Away'

Another monolithic riff is the foundation on which all four musicians are playing in unison part of the time, and then improvising as they go off at their own individual tangents. The ominous air of brooding menace throughout calls The Doors to mind at times, with a similar kind of feel to that of 'Riders on the Storm'. There is little to the lyrics, apart from a brief picture at the start of 'a thousand cities in the night, each one waiting for the light', but some dramatic sci-fi sound effects – crashing boulders, storms, bangs and crashes, in fact, the whole armoury – add atmosphere and punctuate it throughout the passages when all four are holding back on their instruments.

In Rock – Deep Purple

Personnel:
Ian Gillan: vocals
Ritchie Blackmore: guitar
Roger Glover: bass
Jon Lord: organ
Ian Paice: drums
Produced at IBC, De Lane Lea, Abbey Road Studios, all London, October 1969-April 1970 by Deep Purple.
UK release date: June 1970; US release date: August 1970
Record label: Harvest, UK; Warner Bros, US
Highest chart places: UK: 4, US: 143
Running time: 43:30
All songs written by Ritchie Blackmore, Ian Gillan, Roger Glover, Jon Lord and Ian Paice.

After three albums in the late 1960s, the three core members, Blackmore, Lord and Paice, replaced their erstwhile vocalist and bassist with former Episode Six members, Gillan and Glover respectively, and their next project was a fusion of classics and prog rock with Lord's *Concerto for Group and Orchestra*. Blackmore was the one most determined to turn his back on any similar projects in future, and intended that next, they would make a proper rock'n'roll record. If it was not dramatic or exciting, he said, it would have no place on the album. One glance at the Mount Rushmore-inspired cover with the heads of all five members woven into the structure proved that they were out to make a bold impression.

Having been playing several of these numbers on stage for some time, although most if not all of them went through various changes before the final recorded versions, the group had been bursting with ideas before they entered the studio, and they captured everything to perfection. It was the album they had been longing to make, and although several subsequent projects have followed over the ensuing half-century or so, the general view is that they never surpassed this. In Britain, it stayed on the album charts for almost eighteen months and cemented their reputation, second only in the hard rock stakes to Led Zeppelin.

'Speed King'

The opening cut immediately sets the pace. Although not titled separately, the intro was originally a short instrumental, 'Woffle'. It features Blackmore, wrenching all manner of Hendrix-style bombast and feedback from his guitar, then floating into about forty seconds of Lord's soothing organ, almost as if walking from a thunderstorm outside into a church as divine service is beginning. It was inspired by their being used to coming on stage at the start of their show when they had no chance to do a soundcheck first, so to compensate, they deliberately made as much noise as they could, giving the sound engineer a brief chance to adjust the levels before they started playing properly. On the American pressing of the album, it was edited out, lest it should put listeners off – as if any American purchaser was expecting an album by Deep Purple to be anything other than loud. It all changes as Paice and Glover kick the rhythm section into gear, and Gillan's inimitable scream vocal lets loose with a volley of phrases and titles from the Little Richard songbook. Good Golly Miss Molly, Lucille, Tutti Frutti, rockin' in the house of blue light, Saturday night and he just got paid, all reel off the tongue. This is five minutes of full-on power, with drums, organ and guitar pacing themselves and taking their turn during the jam in the middle section of the song, topped by the scream of the man who reminds us he is a 'speed king'. The song was developed and worked on during live shows as it took shape before being recorded, with the initial working title of 'Kneel and Pray'. A first take featured Lord on piano, and appeared as a B-side in Holland.

'Bloodsucker'

Blackmore and Glover originally created this number on acoustic guitars at a session in the former's flat and then developed it with the others at the studio. The guitar riff sounds vaguely 'Whole Lotta Love'-like in places, the Hammond organ alternately takes flight and growls menacingly, there are some very effective stop-start moments, and Gillan screams himself into a frenzy towards the fadeout. Lyrically, it could be about a particularly exploitative woman, or possibly concerning a dispute with the group's manager about an advance payment, hence a reference in the last verse, 'I can find a way to pay you back your twenty pounds'.

'Child in Time'

At ten minutes plus, the album's marathon was one of their longest studio recordings ever. From quiet things, loud things come, as a soft organ and cymbal-tapping intro are followed by Gillan singing what sounds at first like a lullaby, until his controlled scream starts. At four minutes in comes a fast and furious jam led by Blackmore, then stops briefly for Lord to begin again. The second part of the song follows, with Gillan's screaming becoming ever more intense until a positive frenzy of instruments takes over, speeds up and turns into a maelstrom before the final resounding chord. The intro was borrowed from 'Bombay Calling', a jazz instrumental popularised by San Francisco psych group, It's a Beautiful Day the previous year, that Lord had been playing with in the studio and decided to rearrange. Gillan wrote the words, an anti-war song inspired by the conflict in Vietnam. Although far too long to be considered for single release, the track became a favourite on stage, and was eternally popular with fans. Some still regard it to this day as the group's finest piece ever, and during the height of the Iron Curtain tensions in Eastern Europe, it became something of an unofficial anthem for anti-Communist resistance movements.

'Flight of the Rat'

The last song recorded for the album opens side two. It began when Lord was playing around with variations on Rimsky-Korsakov's 'Flight of the Bumble Bee'. For once, Gillan keeps the screaming out of earshot, but the pace throughout is frantic, with organ and then guitar at breakneck pace before going into a funkier mode, underpinned by bass. Everyone gets a chance to take a solo, with another jam session after the end of the song and a drum break to bring almost eight minutes of carefully controlled frenzy to an end.

'Into the Fire'

The only track shy of four minutes, and as such, the only one that was played regularly on radio at the time, has a veiled anti-drug message in the lyrics. According to Paice, it is about 'someone who is making a mistake, taking the wrong plunge'. A grinding riff and some soloing on guitar appear between the verses, although everything is kept short and sweet.

'Living Wreck'

One of the first numbers to be recorded at the sessions, due to the group's initial lack of enthusiasm for the result, it came close to being left off the running order. A mid-tempo number, it is characterised by a fade-in drum start, and whooshing organ sounds vying with guitar. Above all, there are some interesting lyrical turns of phrase, the living wreck apparently being a groupie who took off her hair, pulled out her teeth, and claimed to be a virgin 'full of promise and mystery'.

'Hard Lovin' Man'

Seven minutes' worth at full throttle, much of it at a galloping pace, is the final helping. Pyrotechnics on guitar over a bass riff, which was the original starting point for the number, are joined by a steady rhythm on the drums and organ work, with Lord producing some distinctive passages by hitting as many of the keys simultaneously as possible and a match for the equally frantic vocals. As for the guitar solo, or rather guitar effects that bring it to an end, Blackmore, ever ready to add to his sonic palette by trying out new ideas, achieved these by rubbing his instrument up and down the doorway of the control room because he found the resulting wild noise intriguing. One of the engineers, he said, looked at him as if he had lost his mind.

Full House – Fairport Convention

Personnel:
Richard Thompson: vocals, electric guitar
Dave Swarbrick: vocals, fiddle, viola, mandolin
Simon Nicol: vocals, electric and acoustic guitars, bass, electric dulcimer
Dave Pegg: vocals, bass, mandolin
Dave Mattacks: drums, percussion, harmonium, bodhran
Produced at Sound Techniques Studio, London; Vanguard Studios, New York City,
February-April 1970, by Joe Boyd.
UK and US release date: July 1970
Record label: Island, UK; A&M, US
Highest chart place: UK: 13, did not chart in the US

Having made four albums in the sixties, in 1970, the ever-changing Fairport
Convention found themselves without a female vocalist for the first time. Their
previous set, *Liege and Lief*, had been the start of a conscious move away from
cover versions of contemporary American material, notably songs by Dylan, in
favour of a greater exploration and reinterpretation of songs from the British
folk heritage. It was a path Swarbrick had already taken as one half of a duo
with Martin Carthy a few years earlier. The trend continues here, given added
bite by Thompson's inimitable, biting guitar work and 'sturdy yeoman' vocals,
a contrast to Swarbrick's lighter tones.

While Fairport have long since become part of Britain's post-1950s musical
heritage, with an ever-changing line-up and a suitably lengthy back catalogue
to go with it, even their most ardent fans will admit that they peaked with
their first few albums. Some maintain that *Full House* was their best-ever, and
that they never scaled such heights again. In particular, the interplay between
Thompson and Swarbrick, sometimes playing together, and sometimes
providing a call-and-response routine, is masterful. It was to be the only one
the group ever recorded with this line-up, as Thompson would depart for a
solo career shortly after it was released, leaving Nicol as the only remaining
founder member.

'Walk Awhile' (Thompson, Swarbrick)

The opening track, and one of three compositions by the two frontmen, sets
the tone for the whole record. A crisp instrumental introduction with fiddle on
one channel and guitar on the other, finds them playing more or less in unison,
with snatches of two reels and jigs that abruptly switch tempo before the first
verse, and with bass and drums providing the right amount of gentle bombast
behind them. The song could be almost described as shuffling country rock,
but of a peculiarly English stamp, with all four taking turns to sing the verses
solo and harmonising with each other on the choruses. Whether they had sat
down and carefully written the lyrics beforehand or whether they were trading
lines off the cuff is anybody's guess – I would suspect the latter – but you have

to applaud the eccentricity in couplets like 'Bring along the brewer's head, bring the cuckoo tree, bring your lady mother along to keep us company'. And when you think the song is about to finish, along comes another quick-change tempo with a twenty-second jig.

'Dirty Linen' (traditional)
Just four minutes are all they need to present several tunes woven together, with each member getting a chance to take the spotlight. Swarbrick and Thompson play in unison, then Swarbrick and Pegg on bass offer the same lines while Mattacks lays down his drumsticks to take up the bodhran instead. Pause for an interlude from both guitarists playing acoustically, with barely a pause for breath before violin and electric guitar resume their command duties. The bass and drums start and stop throughout, and by the end, everybody is playing in unison at a dizzy pace. Listen closely and you can hear someone handclapping in time as well. The whole track is a sheer joy yet demands careful attention in order to appreciate how well each segment flows from one to the next

'Sloth' (Thompson, Swarbrick)
The music can go in an instant from joy to the most sombre of moods, as it does on this nine-minute epic. The lyrics (which do not mention the title anywhere) convey, cryptically, an anti-war message, as they tell of a call to the colours and a roll on the drum to the weary soldier, just as he has the misfortune to be abandoned by his loved one. Yet the vocal part, with Swarbrick and Thompson alternating and then harmonising, takes up only two minutes or so at the beginning, before a five-minute instrumental section with a short vocal reprise to conclude. Acoustic guitar and marvellously subtle touches from the rhythm section throughout hold everything together to perfection behind the instruments of the two front men, Thompson's often stabbing guitar sounding particularly fuelled by passion. Verging on prog-folk indeed in its intensity and in its light and shade with full-tilt and more laid-back sections alternating, the whole is doom-laden but compulsive, without ever flagging for a second. The live version was often considerably longer, incorporating a jam session of almost Grateful Dead-like proportions.

'Sir Patrick Spens' (traditional)
This British folk song was one of the Child ballads collected and first published in the 18th century. Its lyrics tell the tale of a sea captain in medieval (or earlier) times who was summoned by the King of Scotland to undertake an errand in midwinter and he undertakes the task reluctantly, knowing there will be a severe storm that could be the end of him. His fears are proved right when he and his crew are drowned off the coast of Aberdeen. The group had already recorded an earlier version during the sessions for *Liege and Lief,* with Sandy Denny singing. With Pegg and Nicol supplying the harmonies, Swarbrick takes lead vocals as well as adding flourishes on fiddle.

'Flatback Caper' (Ronald Cooper, Turlough O'Carolan, traditional)
The vocalists take a rest during six minutes of jigs and reels. It serves as an
ideal showcase for the dual mandolin work of Swarbrick and Pegg, with no
violin or electric guitar to be heard for once. Tunes and tempos change in
quick succession, with Mattacks' drums and Nicol on bass for a change keeping
control through every little switch.

'Doctor of Physick' (Thompson, Swarbrick)
Written very much in the vein of an old traditional song, this slower-paced
number is a brutal tale in which 'Doctor Monk unpacks his trunk tonight'
as he visits young girls. They will realise when they awake the next morning
that their maidenhood is gone. Swarbrick takes centre stage on lead vocals
and viola, while Thompson delivers some suitably savage, understated power
chords, and Mattacks adds some discreet harmonium as well as drums.

'Flowers of the Forest' (traditional)
Ending the album on a dignified air is an old Scottish lament that had been
written to commemorate the defeat of the Scottish army of King James IV
at the battle of Flodden, Northumberland, in 1513. Since then, the tune
has often been played by pipers at memorial services and funerals, among
them that of Queen Victoria in 1901, and it has become known as a tune
that many will not perform in public at any other occasion because of their
reverence for the spirit in which it was written. (It did not prevent the group
from playing it live on Scottish TV some years later, with Nicol informing the
audience that he was half-Scottish himself as he introduced it). Nicol plays
electric dulcimer, providing the drone that would normally come from the
bagpipes, as they give it a suitably respectful performance with peerless four-
part vocal harmonies.

Related Material
Bonus tracks on the 2001 CD reissue included both sides of a 1970
standalone single, 'Now Be Thankful', its B-side, 'Sir B. McKenzie's
Daughter's Lament', and another Thompson-Swarbrick composition –
another song written in traditional style, 'Poor Will and the Jolly Hangman',
in which Thompson sings a slow, mournful number of a man who suffers the
full penalty of the law, with dark humour inherent in the refrain, 'Here's a
toast to the Jolly Hangman, he'll hang you the best that he can'. It includes
a break featuring one of his most jagged guitar solos, with Swarbrick on
mandolin adding sturdy support and particularly prominent drums from
Mattacks. Thompson was dissatisfied with the result; whether unhappy with
his solo, the arrangement or the final mixing, depends on which version
you read. It had been placed in the running order after 'Flatback Caper'
before being removed, but the initial batch of sleeves had been printed, and
a corrected track listing had to be pasted over. Thompson reworked the

recording in 1975, adding backing vocals from his then-wife Linda, and it also subsequently appeared on several anthologies, including his own 1976 compilation of previously unreleased material, *(guitar, vocal)*.

Mungo Jerry – Mungo Jerry

Personnel:
Ray Dorset: vocals, electric, steel, 6 and 12 string acoustic guitars, kazoo, harp, foot stomp, percussion
Paul King: vocals, banjo, 6 and 12 string acoustic guitars, harp, jug, kazoo, jaw's harp
Colin Earl: vocals, piano
Mike Cole: double bass
Johnny Van Derrick: violin
Produced at Pye Studios, London, December 1969, by Barry Murray.
UK release date: July 1970; US release date, August 1970
Record label: Dawn, UK; Janus, US
Highest chart places: UK: 14 US: 64
Running time: 41:12

Hot on the heels of the Hollywood festival and a subsequent number one single that completely dominated the nation's airwaves that long hot summer in Britain with music press headlines of 'Mungomania', the material on Mungo Jerry's debut album was taken, like the three tracks from the maxi-single (none of which were duplicated on the original British release), from sessions at the end of the previous year (in the wintertime, in fact) at which seventeen tracks had been laid down. All members had been much influenced by good-time blues, skiffle, folk, jug band music and rockabilly, it was inevitable that this would be a blend of all genres. There is so much energy to be heard throughout this album that it is easy to forget the group did not have a drummer in those early days. Ray Dorset compensated for that in the studio with his miked-up foot stomp and occasional overdubbed percussion, and a washboard player generally accompanied them on stage. As for the packaging, British buyers were treated to a three-dimensional red and green viewer with which to look at the group photo on the inner gatefold section. (The same device also works on plenty of other albums, by the way).

'In the Summertime' was added to overseas releases, either as a bonus track or else instead of 'Tramp' or 'Daddie's Brew', to boost sales potential. In some territories, it was accordingly titled *In the Summertime*. British non-singles buyers had to wait for it until 1971 and the group's second LP, *Electronically Tested*.

Songs about nuclear warfare and down-and-outs apart, this was good-time music personified and one of the most carefree albums of the year. As *New Musical Express* commented approvingly in its review, 'Entertainment is back'. Frontman Dorset had always been the driving force, a situation that would result in King's departure after two more albums, but this was a first-rate calling card for the talent as well as the spirit that they collectively brought to the table.

'Baby Let's Play House' (Arthur Gunter)

Originally made famous by Elvis Presley in 1955 during his Sun label days, this hits top gear immediately. Dorset's earthy voice, doing a marvellous Elvis impersonation, and guitar are totally swamped in echo to great effect. Earl pounds the ivories in wildest Jerry Lee Lewis-style, with one extraordinary break near the end where the keys pan from one stereo channel to the other. On early gigs, he had played his own honky tonk piano, a small Eavestaff instrument, with drawing pins added to the key hammers to give it a barroom sound and increase the volume. In the Pye studio, he also had the choice of a Steinway grand, and usually overdubbed his solos so that on some tracks – this being a good example – the sound jumps out at the listener.

'Johnny B. Badde' (Dorset)

No prizes for guessing what inspired a title like this. It is typical of the infectious jug band numbers that made up much of the group's set at this time. Wild wailing harmonica dominates the introduction, while piano and banjo are both prominent in the mix, until towards the end, they fade into the distance and leave King's jug to take us out.

'San Francisco Bay Blues' (Jesse Fuller)

A song much-loved by many folk and blues artists since the mid-1950s, this is driven throughout by piano, with Dorset's vocals sounding more than ever like one of the vintage bluesmen. King's jaw's harp and jug are both heard in the intro, and both kazoos are playing against each other, both at different pitches. Can you have kazoos in harmony? This proves you can.

'Sad Eyed Joe' (King)

Whereas Dorset contributed the more straight-down-the-line rockers and blues numbers, King's speciality was for the lighter, more folk-influenced songs, that melody-wise generally pushed well beyond the three-chord barrier. Both vocalists had the vibrato that Marc Bolan also made famous at around this time, but with King's songs, there was also a touch of Donovan-style gentle whimsicality. Although it is the gloomy story of a man who leaves his family to go out into the mountains prospecting for gold and is eventually found lying frozen at the bottom of the creek, it still has a characteristically up-tempo sound, given added colour not only by piano and unobtrusive lead guitar but also harmonica and Van Derrick's violin.

Maggie (Dorset)

Another three-chord stomper, this runs the whole gamut of kazoo, harmonica and pounding keys ('let's hear that piano, boy', Dorset calls out at one point), with some neat touches of rockabilly lead guitar, all topped by the slightly bawdy vocal. You can see and almost hear that lascivious twinkle in his eye as he sings. Ever since their first gig at Oxford University, it had always gone down particularly well on stage, and it was issued as a single in France and Norway.

'Peace in the Country' (Dorset)

The album's most sombre moment takes a brief excursion into social comment. Although the music is still bright and breezy piano, harmonica and kazoo, plus a few touches of violin, the lyrics are about the spectre of nuclear conflict. Millions have died, the lyrics tell us, nuclear warheads are flying all around, and there are no fish left in the ocean, no birds in the sea. There is an effective moment just over halfway through when all the instruments apart from violin cut out behind Dorset's vocal, as he sings chillingly that somebody dropped the bomb.

'See Me' (Dorset)

Side two starts with the least restrained number of all. The lyrics are lasciviously simple, but nobody is going to analyse Dorset's prowess as a wordsmith on what he admits is a 'wild and over the top' song unashamedly influenced by Captain Beefheart. A fest for lead guitar, distorted screaming and growling, plus kazoo and harmonica running riot just as much as the piano, mean this may not be one for the faint-hearted.

'Movin' On' (King)

The second of King's paeans to freedom and the joys of life in the open air sings of trading in the tedium of working in a factory and savouring the great outdoors instead. All is well until the police find him sleeping on the beach and tell him he has 'gotta move on'. Piano, acoustic guitar and wonderful hoedown violin provide the main accompaniment.

'My Friend' (Dorset)

Introducing an attractive woman who insists that everybody is her friend and invites the narrator who cannot resist her to come and have a drink on her. In a scenario reminiscent of The Beatles' 'Norwegian Wood', to take just one example, he takes her home, and everything is fine until he wakes up the next morning to find that she and every penny he had the night before have all gone. Lead and slide guitar plus kazoos add to the jollity of a slightly cruel song.

'Mother*!*!*! Boogie' (Dorset, King, Earl, Cole)

What blues group cannot resist an occasional twelve-bar jam in the studio? All four members take turns with piano leading the proceedings, occasionally slowing down for a bar or two. Stand-up bass wanders up and down the scale, twelve-string guitars and harmonicas cut loose and boldly go anywhere in the playground they please. In the hands of many another group, it might have continued for ten minutes or more, but here it is kept to a little under three. The genuine title (little imagination needed) has since appeared in print elsewhere, mainly in other reviews, but there were limits to the printed word in 1970.

'Tramp' (King)

The only number to break the five-minute barrier comes in King's third wistful contribution. Some folksy finger-picking on acoustic guitar and poignant violin accompany this sketch, set to a tune dominated by minor chords, of an elderly man on the streets, whose bed is the pavement, whose dreams fade away as he sleeps, and who searches through the dustbins for food.

'Daddie's Brew' (Earl)

The final track is the sole contribution from Earl, singing in a voice richly embedded in echo, pumping the keys with the merest touch of lead guitar and bass, as he delivers a lighthearted country-meets-blues song that suggests the influence of Jerry Lee Lewis and others. Daddie makes his own special brew in a still hidden in the wood (the wild west during the prohibition era, perhaps?), far stronger than anything his friends, acquaintances or the revenue man can handle.

Signed, Sealed and Delivered – Stevie Wonder

Personnel:
Stevie Wonder: lead and backing vocals, harmonica, drums, percussion, keyboards
The Andantes, Wonderlove, The Originals: backing vocals
Bob Babbitt: bass
Eddie Wills: sitar
Richard 'Pistol' Allen: drums
The Funk Brothers: all other instruments
Recorded 1969-70.
Produced at Hitsville USA, Detroit, 1969-70, by Stevie Wonder, Henry Cosby, Ron Miller, Steve Marcel Bega.
UK and US release date: August 1970
Record label: Tamla Motown, UK; Tamla, US
Highest chart place: Did not chart in the UK, US: 25
Running time: 35:12.

By the time the child star formerly known as Little Stevie Wonder turned 20 in 1970, with over a dozen albums (three of them live) to his credit, he was allowed to co-produce as well as co-write his own records. On his twelfth studio outing, six of the twelve tracks found him collaborating with other writers, including his mother Lula Mae Hardaway and his future wife Syreeta Wright. At a time when several of the more bankable Tamla Motown hitmakers were either splintering or even leaving the company, it was fortunate for them that some of their other acts were developing, and none more so than Wonder. Four of the tracks were also hit singles, and they are placed at the start of the running order.

All in all, the album is a step forward for Wonder and also for the Detroit sound. Four very strong singles, and a more eclectic sound palette that found him experimenting as a songwriter and co-producer with funk, ballads, gospel and the pop-soul sound on which the Motown heritage had been largely founded a few years previously, hinted at the musical force that he was about to become. Although it has its darker, melancholic moments, much of it is savours of a joyous frame of mind.

'Never Had a Dream Come True' (Wonder, Henry Cosby, Sylvia Moy)

The most successful single in Britain but the least at home reaching 26 and six respectively, this romantic mid-tempo number with a hint of country style, in which Wonder sings of love for a girl evidently just out of reach, is buoyed along with sympathetic strings and piano, and robust guitar. Some of his songs in this vein had a tendency to become cloying, but this one avoids falling into the trap.

We Can Work It Out (Lennon, McCartney)

Wonder had always admired The Beatles as people and musicians, especially after his first meeting with McCartney in 1966 after a gig in London. This is a real masterclass in taking a Beatles song, tweaking it gently in places, adapting it to a different genre, and still sounding just as good. Some critics maintain that it is even better than the Fab Four version, maybe even the best Lennon-McCartney cover of all time. Musically it sounds not unlike an energetic first cousin of his first top ten hit of three years earlier, 'I Was Made To Love Her', with its bold electric piano, vigorous backing vocals, bustling tambourine, and trademark jazz-inflected harmonica. It is all taken at quite a funky pace, and dispenses with the little waltz-time 'fussing and fighting my friend' interludes heard on the original.

'Signed, Sealed, Delivered (I'm Yours)' (Lee Garrett, Hardaway, Wonder, Wright)

Opening up with a descending riff on sitar, this similarly joyous piece of infectiously bouncy funk leads into a groove-driven along by the combination of insistent horns, a bubbling rhythm section, and lively backing vocals. As the title track of the album, it became the highest-charting of the singles in its home territory, charting at three in the USA and fifteen in the UK.

'Heaven Help Us All' (Ron Miller)

A more sombre mood arrives at this point, a world-weary number about seeking solace in faith in an unforgiving world. Although it was not one of those which he helped to write, it marked the start of commentary in his music on social concerns such as racism, homelessness, poverty and the futility of war, as he muses about helping the downtrodden: 'heaven help the black man if he struggles one more day, heaven help the white man if he turns by the way'. A gospel-style choir from the backing vocalists enhances the mood. It was the lowest-charting of the British singles at only 29, although it reached number nine in the US.

'You Can't Judge a Book By Its Cover' (Cosby, Pam Sawyer, Wonder)

Not so much a song, more a groove built around the title, this is similar in approach to the Isley Brothers' hit of the previous year (and their first after leaving Motown), 'It's Your Thing'. With its clavinet and bass riff, gritty lead guitar and throbbing bass, it works up a storm as Wonder contemplates on how appearances can often be deceptive – 'you can't judge a love by its lover', runs another line. Strong on energy, it is less so on melody.

'Sugar' (Don Hunter)

Another number built around a warm groove, this features the horns punching out lines and lead guitar curling round the vocals, as Wonder sings himself into a frenzy of ecstasy. He tells us he has no need for fancy places, or cannon and wine (an interesting pairing), as all he wants is good home cooking and some sugar after suppertime (best left to the imagination), his singing becoming ever more ecstatic as he reaches the end. A move upwards in key towards the end adds a note of interest.

'Don't Wonder Why' (Leonard Caston)

Side two opens with the longest number on the album, at almost five minutes. A lovelorn ballad that touches smooth R'n'B, gospel and even jazz, it opens with slow, portentous work on the piano, underpinned by dark strings, rather like the sound of an early Elton John tune. In the lyrics, the rejected lover is passed by, his partner apparently not even seeing him, while the nights grow old and winds blow cold. During the break, strings and harmonica vie for attention.

'Anything You Want Me To Do' (Hunter, Hardaway, Paul Riser, Wonder)

One of inevitably a quota of so-so numbers in a poppy style, this mid-tempo love song moves along with a sturdy bass figure and brass section as he sings to his lover how much he wants them to get back together and he will do anything. Again, there is a subtle shift up one key near the end, but that apart, it rather lacks interest.

'I Can't Let My Heaven Walk Away' (Joe Hinton, Sawyer)

Much the same applies to this soulful lament on similar lines as he sadly contemplates the end of a love affair, 'Heaven' being the girl to whom he is saying goodbye – 'Only an hour ago I held her in real flesh and blood, she just grabbed her coat and said please I've had enough'. A brief harmonica break that as ever could be nobody but Wonder spices the song up a little, yet even so the result is pleasant but little more.

'Joy (Takes Over Me)' (Duke Browner)

This is a much more upbeat, celebratory song, on which the rhythm section cooks, while Wonder's harmonica battles it out with brass and backing vocals in the break.

'I Gotta Have a Song' (Hunter, Hardaway, Riser, Wonder)

Here is Wonder's soulful affirmation that his passion for music will always get him through the hard times. Once again, he has been unlucky in love, as he sings of having 'no place to be, no-one's needing me, my girl just said we're through.' All he needs is his art; 'Show me to where there's music'. It has a curious melody dominated largely by jazzy-flavoured minor chords, and an arresting intro of single stabbing guitar phrases before flowing into a mid-tempo number with subtle horns and backing vocals prominent above all.

'Something To Say' (Hunter, Wonder)

Another upbeat love song with an optimistic mood ends the collection. A sturdy bass figure plus pounding drums and horns carry this one well, in addition to another striking harmonica break. Bustling soul meets jazz, with echoes of the earlier hit 'My Cherie Amour', and a subtle key change near the end. It makes a satisfying number with which to close.

Cosmo's Factory – Creedence Clearwater Revival

Personnel:
John Fogerty: lead and backing vocals, lead guitar, keyboards, saxophone, harmonica
Tom Fogerty: rhythm guitar, backing vocals
Stu Cook: bass, backing vocals
Doug Clifford: drums
Produced at Wally Heider Studios, San Francisco, 1969-70, by John Fogerty.
UK release date: August 1970; US release date: July 1970
Record label: Liberty, UK: Fantasy, US
Highest chart places: UK: 1, US: 1
Running time: 42:28

The demise of The Beatles left two prime contenders for 'the greatest rock'n'roll band', the Rolling Stones and Creedence Clearwater Revival. For just over a year, the San Francisco quartet issued peerless single after single in quick succession, followed by albums that were almost greatest hits collections, and none more so than their fifth. Most of the eleven tracks were potential singles – and several of them (one admittedly severely edited) duly became A and B sides.

Sadly, this was not only Creedence's best-selling album by far but also their finale as a quartet. They were a time bomb waiting to explode. Internal tensions between the Fogerty brothers, and after the elder's departure between the younger one and his rhythm section, resulted in a gradual implosion after two more LPs. Let us remember them above all for this, which everyone generally agrees showed them at the peak of their powers – or should we call them a one-man-band with the Midas touch who was able to keep the remaining musicians, one his elder brother, on side just long enough before the chemistry corroded?

'Ramble Tamble' (Fogerty)

The one track that was too different to be considered as a 45 comes at the beginning. Basically, it is one very short song, with a lengthy jam in the middle. Starting with a brisk guitar riff played to a rockabilly shuffle, Fogerty delivers a tune that basically revolves around one chord, targeting in a less than specific way contemporary political forces and the evils of government as he sings about police on the corner, the mortgage on the car, and actors in the white house. Two minutes in, it gradually slows down to a brief halt and changes tempo completely for the next three minutes or so for a mid-tempo instrumental section based around four chords, a little reminiscent of the interlude in Cream's 'Badge'. It speeds up towards the end, finishing on a short reprise of the opening rockabilly section and one of the verses at the start, before cruising into another slowdown and finish.

'Before You Accuse Me' (Elias McDaniel)

Although seven of the songs are the work of John Fogerty, they also pay tribute to three of the old rock'n'roll and blues songs that had influenced them as they were growing up. This is a lively romp through an early Bo Diddley tune, with a splendidly swaggering guitar solo and playful piano work.

'Travelin' Band' (Fogerty)

Bring on the greatest hits jukebox, with a two-minute-long number about a group's life on the road. Its opening line, 'Seven-thirty-seven comin' out of the sky' was a reference to the Boeing 737 plane that was being brought into service at the time, and the resigned 'baggage gone, oh well', a reference to their luggage continually getting lost while they were on tour. Top ten on both sides of the Atlantic, it was one of the most infectious rock'n'roll numbers on the album, alive with atmosphere and featuring not only the singer's spine-tingling guitar solo but also piano and saxophone. A couple of years later, Little Richard's record label, Specialty, brought a case for plagiarism, claiming that it was a copy of 'Good Golly Miss Molly' (which Creedence had covered on their second album), leading to an out-of-court settlement.

'Ooby Dooby' (Wade Moore, Dick Penner)

A more or less note-for-note cover of the early Roy Orbison hit follows, with plenty of echo on Fogerty's voice. While it adds nothing to the original, it shows how effectively the group had taken the Sun rock'n'roll sound and brought it to a new generation.

'Lookin' Out My Back Door' (Fogerty)

Almost pure country and another single (reaching number two in the US), one more in a line of hits that fell one short of topping the American chart, this song features some neat pedal steel guitar and a brief slowdown in tempo for a couple of lines towards the end. Fogerty wrote it partly as a children's song, specifically for his three-year-old son. As the title suggests, it begins as a 'good to be home again after being on the road' type of number. There are also references to watching a street circus – 'tambourines and elephants are playin' in the band', inspired by his reading a Dr Seuss book as a child. Some, including Vice-President Spiro Agnew, took exception to a line about 'taking a ride on the flying spoon', which they assumed was about cocaine. Always firmly anti-drugs, the group insisted that it really referred to the silver spoon generally given to a child by its grandmother.

'Run Through the Jungle' (Fogerty)

Opening and closing with jungle sound effects created through multi-tracked guitar and piano played back in reverse, this was assumed to be a song about the Vietnam war. It was, however, about an equally serious contemporary issue; Fogerty stressed it was about American society, and the proliferation of handguns as well as the ease with which they could be purchased. He said he was not anti-gun himself, but uneasy about the lack of firearm control. The whole song is played on one chord throughout, but such is the build-up of dense sound, use of effects and little touches like the wailing harmonica break, that it never flags for a moment.

'Up Around the Bend' (Fogerty)

Side two opens with the song that gave them their greatest British success off the album, for once charting even slightly higher than in America, at number three as opposed to four in the UK. Starting with a simple but irresistibly infectious and distinctive guitar hook, arguably their best-ever, the idea came to Fogerty while he was riding his motorcycle through the hills of California – a joyous summery song about leaving 'the sinking ship behind' and getting away from everything, preferably with your friends – 'always time for a good conversation, there's an ear for what you say'. In Britain, it was sometimes misconstrued as being a lyric about going mad, and he had to explain that it was about looking forward to things in a difficult world getting better 'just around the bend'.

'My Baby Left Me' (Arthur Crudup)

Another nod to Creedence's rock'n'roll influences comes with a short but sweet version of the song that originally put Elvis Presley on the map. Like 'Ooby Dooby', it is superbly executed, although one might be forgiven for wondering why they needed to do their own rendition when it does little more than replicate the original, Fogerty's distinctive voice apart.

'Who'll Stop the Rain' (Fogerty)

A more sombre moment comes in the album's most folksy number. Some maintain that it was Fogerty's statement about the war in Vietnam, to which he replied that he was 'talking about Washington'. It was also partly about their having been at the Woodstock festival where they played a blinding set, and where he watched the crowds getting really muddy and cold when it began to rain, huddling together for warmth. There are also references to political uncertainty, the failures of 'good men through the ages', and 'five-year plans and new deals wrapped in golden chains'.

'I Heard It Through the Grapevine' (Norman Whitfield, Barrett Strong)

Eleven minutes, just over half of side two, are taken up with this marathon number. Fans are divided about its merits, some regarding it as overlong and overblown, while others see it as one of the best-ever workouts of a soul standard by a rock group. Yet unlike the album's other covers, this

has a very different character from the familiar Marvin Gaye recording.
Here is a rock band paying due reverence to a classic song, but making it
completely their own and having the time of their lives without destroying
it. They rehearsed it for several weeks before recording, although there was
a measure of spontaneity each time in the way that all four musicians fed off
each other, trading and repeating little phases as they went on. A four-minute
edit was released as a single about five years later to promote a greatest hits
compilation, long after the group had disbanded, with minor chart success.

'Long as I Can See the Light' (Fogerty)

The record bows out with a tune that offers a complete contrast to the main
body of Creedence's work. One would never have thought of them as a soul
or gospel band, but this comes remarkably close to the genre. Guitar is little
in evidence, and the main accompaniment to this soulful ballad, apart from
the rhythm section, is provided by Fogerty's electric piano and saxophone,
making it almost a solo track. Doug Clifford called it 'a great love song,'
while acknowledging that the word 'love' did not show up in any Creedence
song. Fogerty called it a song about the loner inside him, 'wanting to feel
understood, needing those at home to shine a light', hence his metaphor in the
first line about putting a candle in the window. In America, it was the B-side
of 'Lookin' Out My Back Door' and listed separately as a smaller hit in its own
right, but an A-side in Britain. Fogerty never played it live with the group but
many years later performed a breathtaking orchestral version on which he
played a guitar solo in the break, while leaving the rest of the accompaniment
to strings and brass.

Get Yer Ya-Yas Out! – The Rolling Stones

Personnel:
Mick Jagger: vocals, harmonica
Keith Richards: guitar, backing vocals
Mick Taylor: guitar
Bill Wyman: bass
Charlie Watts: drums
Ian Stewart: piano
Recorded 26-28 November 1969 live, New York City and Baltimore, Maryland,
overdubs at Olympic Studios, London, January-February 1970.
Produced by The Rolling Stones, Glyn Johns.
UK and US release date: September 1970
Record label: Decca, UK; London, US
Highest chart places: UK: 1, US: 6
Running time: 47:36
All songs written by Mick Jagger and Keith Richards, unless stated otherwise.

The Rolling Stones' first official live album, and their last fully-sanctioned
release for Decca Records excluding greatest hits collections and unofficial
compilations, comprised performances from their American tour of
November 1969. It was issued partly to combat the existence of *Live-r
Than You'll Ever Be*, a bootleg made up with an almost identical track
also recorded on the tour but at a gig in California earlier that month. Its
producers claimed that, although illegal, it had sold about 250,000 copies by
the end of 1970.

   The title was taken from a Blind Boy Fuller song. Apart from their versions
of two Chuck Berry classics, it comprised their last two hits and three tracks
each from the previous two studio albums, *Beggars Banquet* and *Let It Bleed*.
This tour was also the first since guitarist Mick Taylor had replaced Brian
Jones, who died soon after being replaced. Now freed from having been –
rather like The Beatles in their final years – a studio-bound unit relying to
some extent on guest backing vocalists and outside musicians, plus Keith
Richards overdubbing much of the bass as well as different guitar parts,
they were newly fired up, raring to get out on stage. It was also the group's
last tour as a sextet, with 'sixth Stone' Ian Stewart on piano, but without
additional singers and brass, horns or keyboard players.

   This album has its flaws, despite Jagger returning to the studio to add
a few vocal overdubs to most of the tracks a few weeks after the initial
recording. Some fans insist that the bootleg was slightly superior, but even
so, this stands up as one of the most acclaimed live albums of all time, and
is regarded as not only the group's first, but by far the best. The group were
definitely on a roll, excuse pun, at the time and showed that on a good night,
they could rock as hard as anyone. It was also the first live album to top the
British charts.

'Jumpin' Jack Flash'
Their 1968 British chart-topper would be a frequent opening number in setlists for years to come, and here they extract every ounce of energy with which they had injected the single. It might be noted that unlike The Who's *Live at Leeds*, on the whole, they stay fairly close to the original recorded versions of their songs, given the constraints of having no extra hired hands or friends as they had in the studio. A further difference between both records is that the Stones include some stage banter and off-the-cuff chat in between tracks. After the applause has died down, Jagger teases female members of the audience with comments about his having lost a button on his trousers and suggesting tongue-in-cheek that they might not like to see what would happen if they were to fall down.

'Carol' (Chuck Berry)
The first of two Chuck Berry numbers, this was one of the standout tracks from their first album in 1964 and a regular favourite throughout the years. Here they play it pretty straight as homage to one of their heroes.

'Stray Cat Blues'
This is proficient enough, but somehow lacks the menacing swagger of the *Beggars Banquet* version. It does tend to give the impression that they are going through the crowd-pleasing motions of 'another track from one of our old LPs'. The original sounded a little faster, less lethargic, and thanks to a searing guitar break it takes up almost the last two minutes without outstaying its welcome for a second, thus almost a minute longer than the slightly disappointing in-concert cut here.

'Love in Vain' (Robert Johnson)
A marvellously mournful blues is the nearest to a ballad that the record comes. One might miss Ry Cooder's wonderful mandolin work from the *Let It Bleed* version, but Richards and Taylor compensate by giving it their all during the break. On the album credits on the initial UK release, the credits read 'traditional, arranged Jagger, Richards', while in the US, the traditional tag was dropped. On *Let It Bleed*, the writer was given as Woody Payne, an alias sometimes used by seminal 1930s bluesman Robert Johnson.

'Midnight Rambler'
To conclude side one, Jagger picks up his harmonica for this nine-minute epic. A brisk boogie is laid down by guitars, bass and drums, later to relax things for a couple of changes in time signatures – to say nothing of further harmonica licks along the way, it is easy to see how this one had the crowd going. Both guitarists bring all the drama they can to the lengthy slow passage around halfway through before roaring back into the boogie for a final breathless surge.

'Sympathy for the Devil'

Turn over, and ignoring demands from someone in the crowd calling out repeatedly for 'Paint It Black', next they launch into the standout number from *Beggars Banquet*. For those of us who believe that the original studio version was one of their best pieces ever, this is a prime example of how six minutes of magic on tape or vinyl can often never really be recreated on stage. Cue a couple of guitar chords, a stroke on the cymbal, and they are under way in front of the crowds. Gone is that subtle beat on the congas, the dervish-like cries, and – ah, sacrilege – the eerie 'hoo-hoo' refrain from the third verse onwards. The Madison Square Gardens audience were doubtless content with what they heard and saw, but this time Lucifer simply does not sound like the devil-crazed demon of yore.

'Live With Me'

Some of the same criticisms can be made of the next track, which in its original studio incarnation was as tight as they come, building up from a few seconds on bass and then drums before the vocals pitch in. Jagger again seems to be coasting rather than snarling out his lyrics with venom. Richards and Taylor supply suitably crazed guitars during the break, but it fails to compensate for the absence of Bobby Keys's masterful sax, both here and in the fadeout. As in 'Stray Cat Blues', this is noticeably shorter than the studio version, coming to an abrupt end on the final chorus.

'Little Queenie' (Berry)

'Ah New York City, you talk a lot, let's have a look at you,' Jagger calls out as the rhythm guitar roars into action for a second visit to the Chuck Berry songbook. This packs more of a punch than 'Carol', Stewart being more in evidence as he hammers on the piano keys. Having said that, meanwhile, I was thinkin' … the Stones sound a little slow on this. A quick listen to a couple of Berry's performances of the same song, recorded several years apart, only reinforces this view.

'Honky Tonk Women'

At this time, what was and would always remain the group's most successful single, in Britain at least (five weeks atop the charts one summer earlier), is kept for near the end of the record, after a quick 'Charlie's good tonight, inne?' That would become a much-loved catchphrase, referring to the drummer (or maybe something else beginning with C). This time, you scarcely miss the horns from the original or the cowbell at the start. In the break, both guitarists and pianist pull out all the stops. Also, for the sharp-eared, Jagger sings a second verse that is not on the single, about 'Strollin' on the boulevards of Paris.' Just for the record, on the live double album released at about the same time, 'Mad Dogs and Englishmen', Joe Cocker's version of the same song boasts three verses – all of which have completely different lyrics from both Stones versions.

'Street Fighting Man'

Last comes the number that had been an American single in 1968 but was banned by some radio stations for being too subversive after anti-Vietnam war riots in Chicago. It also became the first of three tracks on a British maxi-single the following year, after the group had left Decca. The slightly longer lead break that brings it to a finish is a bonus, not least when one guitar breaks into a few seconds of the intro to 'You Really Got Me'.

Right: The Beatles at Tittenhurst Park, August 1969, together reluctantly for the last time at a photoshoot. (*Croydon Music Archives*)

Left: Jimi Hendrix, whose sudden death in September left the music world in mourning.

Right: Steve Winwood (left) of Traffic with the band Free, relaxing in Amsterdam while touring Europe together in July. (*Wikipedia Creative Commons*)

Melody Maker

JUNE 13, 1970   1s weekly   USA 25 cents

Vote next week — for music

NEXT THURSDAY, Britain goes to the polls to decide who will govern the country for the next five years. And on the same day, MM readers will have the chance to register a vote for their favourite groups, musicians, singers, and records in the world-famous Melody Maker Pop Poll.

Like the General Election, our poll has the whole scene buzzing with the news of its results, and particularly its upsets.

Remember last year, when Christine Perfect shot in from nowhere to capture the British girl singer's award?

Your votes will decide how she, and her contemporaries, fare this year.

It's no secret that, over the past couple of years, the pop scene has reached a degree of sophistication unparalleled in its history.

The emergence as major forces of bands like Blood, Sweat and Tears, Chicago, Ginger Baker's Air Force and the Soft Machine is eloquent testimony to the fact that pop fans are now more interested in the music than the image.

In keeping with this trend, the MM has improved its poll, so that it now includes several new categories.

This will create considerable interest inside and outside the music business, and enhance the reputation which the MM poll already has. VOTE NEXT WEEK!

IT'S MUNGOMANIA!

SUMMERTIME PINTS for a hot hit group. From left: Mike Cole, Paul King, Ray Dorset and Colin Earl

MUNGO JERRY MANIA STRIKES! And in the middle of it, two members of the band flew away on Tuesday for holidays.

With their single, "In The Summertime," jumping from number 23 to 5 in the MM chart — and selling at a rate of 40,000 a day last week — bassist Paul King and pianist Colin Earl this week took themselves away to Ibiza and Greece.

So the group, who hit the headlines with their crowd-pleasing appearance at the recent Hollywood Festival, will all be on holiday until their next date — on June 20 at the Hamburg Festival.

On June 24 they return to Britain for one nighters which include Keele University (26), Crawley (25), New Century Hall, Manchester (27), Cleethorpes (28), and Town Hall, High Wycombe (30).

Their London debut will be held back to the middle of July, when they appear at the Lyceum to coincide with the release on July 17 of their first album on the Dawn label.

The album will have a 3-D cover, with a pair of free special spectacles through which to look.

Who set for Isle of Wight

THE WHO will be back at the Isle of Wight this year — and Chicago are planning to record their next album "live" at the festival.

Having topped the bill on the Saturday night last year, the Who will again be playing on the Saturday, August 29.

Festival promoter Ron Foulk told the MM that 1970's event will be much bigger than the previous one, and already he has a staff of 30 working on the administration.

Tickets for the festival will go on sale towards the end of the month.

● THE WHO in America: KEITH MOON reports to the MM on page 36.

How Miles Davis went pop

TURN TO PAGE 20

Left: Mungomania dominates the midsummer singles chart, while Dylan releases another chart-topping (if critically panned) album.

Melody Maker

SEPTEMBER 5, 1970   1s weekly   USA 25 cents

Isle of Wight special
JETHRO TOUR

And no more singles?

Joni's triumph

JONI MITCHELL scored a notable personal triumph at the Isle of Wight. Despite two disturbing interruptions — one by a fan and one by a gentleman who grabbed the mike between songs and tried to blurt out a message to the "revolutionaries" — she overcame her considerable nervousness and stunned the crowd with a set full of peerlessly beautiful songs, leaving to an ovation after several encores. Neil Young, who accompanied Joni to the island, was set to make a guest appearance on Saturday night, but left quickly — he was reported to have been upset by the festival's overall atmosphere. Full festival coverage begins on page 24.

JETHRO TULL start a 12-day tour of Britain on September 23.

It is their first British tour since the beginning of 1969, and their first with the new five-man line-up including new pianist John Evan. They will be supported by Procol Harum, who will be playing virtually their only British dates this year, and Tir Na Nog, a folk duo from Ireland.

The tour includes three midnight shows in Birmingham, Glasgow and Manchester.

Speaking about the tour, Jethro leader Ian Anderson told the MM this week: "The problem of playing in England is that most of the places only hold about 2,000 people and tickets are soon sold out. So we are trying to do two shows. There is so much happening in these halls that we could only get in at midnight, which rather limits the number of people who can go, but is better than not playing at all.

"There will be no new records to coincide with the tour, though the group should have their next album released in about January. I don't think we will make any more singles," said Ian. "I don't think we need a chart single now and if we did do one it would be an album track. After the English tour we go back to America for a short tour and then we will start recording for the next album."

The three midnight shows are at Birmingham Town Hall on September 25 when the three groups will play two houses — one at 7.30 p.m. and another from midnight to 3 a.m. At the Queen's Playhouse, Glasgow, on October 2 and at the Free Trade Hall, Manchester, on October 3, they will play one three hour show starting at midnight.

Other dates are Sheffield City Hall (September 23), Albert Hall, Nottingham (24), City Hall, Newcastle (27), De Montfort Hall, Leicester (28), Music Hall, Aberdeen (30), Caird Hall, Dundee (October 1), Colston Hall, Bristol (4), Guildhall, Southampton (9) and Albert Hall, London (13).

TODAY'S MUSIC GIANTS TALK TO THE MM . . .

Alvin Lee
SPECIAL INTERVIEW ON PAGE 16

Leonard Cohen
THE POET SPEAKS ON PAGE 11

Jimi Hendrix
ON HIS NEW BAND — SEE PAGE 7

Soft Machine
A CLASSICAL GAS? — SEE PAGE 15

Mingus for Britain

CHARLES MINGUS, one of the most controversial figures in jazz, stars at Ronnie Scott's Club in London for three weeks from November 9.

"It will be his first time here, and he will be with his new quintet," Ronnie Scott told the MM on Tuesday.

"And opposite him I have booked a very good group I heard early last week, Mark-Almond."

Because of other commitments, Mingus will not play the club on November 20 and 21, when the Buddy Rich Orchestra will take over the stand. There will be two shows by Rich each night—from 8 to 11 p.m. and 12 midnight to 3 a.m.

Meanwhile, Ronnie Scott has a string of other top jazz names fixed for the club. And he is hoping to present Tony Williams Lifetime "sometime in October or late September," adds Scott. "At least for one or two nights, and possibly a week."

Scott is trying to get jazz violinist Stephane Grappelly

for a season at the club in December. (Grappelly was a big hit on BBC-2's filming of a Scott Club TV session last week.)

Tenorist Dexter Gordon is set for a fortnight from September 28. Playing opposite is American singer Esther Marrow. "I heard her in the States and she is really excellent," says Ronnie.

The Clarke-Boland Big Band returns to the club for two weeks from October 12. The Elvin Jones Quartet, plus Salena Jones, are there on October 26 for two weeks. Earl Hines and his Quintet play from November 30 to December 12.

Currently, The Stars of Faith and the Alan Haven Trio are playing Scott's.

CHARLES MINGUS: First time in Britain

Left: Joni Mitchell, the major success story of the Isle of Wight festival in August.

Left: Edwin Starr, whose 'War' was as powerful an indictment of the Vietnam war as the singles chart ever experienced.

Right: Errol Brown, the voice and face of Hot Chocolate, one of Britain's most consistent singles acts from 1970 onwards.

Left: Fairport Convention, the indestructible founding fathers of British folk-rock.

Right: The Tremeloes, pop-rock veterans whose reputation suffered after an ill-advised press interview. Sometimes, silence really is golden.

Left: Black Sabbath, heavy metal trailblazers who gave the Vertigo label their first top 10 single and number one album.

Right: Keith Emerson, ELP's keyboard maestro, often seen as the godfather of prog rock.

Left: Marmalade, reluctant 60s pop stars who insisted on total artistic control with their second record deal - and got it.

Right: The Rolling Stones, who entered the 70s with Britain's first number one live album.

Left: The Who, whose *Live at Leeds* was hailed at the time as 'the definitive hard rock holocaust'.

Right: Traffic, reluctant psychedelic hitmakers who embraced folk-rock with their reunion album *John Barleycorn Must Die*.

Left: McGuinness Flint, dressed as Victorian undertakers on Dartmoor for the sleeve of their debut album.

Right: The Moody Blues, asking 'questions' about hate and death and war.

Left: Fleetwood Mac, whose 'The Green Manalishi' marked the end of the Peter Green (second from left) era.

Right: Edison Lighthouse, whose 'Love Grows' was one of several simultaneous hits to feature Tony Burrows on vocal.

Left: *Moondance* by Van Morrison. A moderate success on first release, and later said to be arguably the best album of Van Morrison's long career. (*Warner Bros/Warner Music Group*)

Right: *Bridge Over Troubled Water* by Simon and Garfunkel. A record-breaking 33 weeks (non-consecutive) at number one and the best-selling album in Britain during the 70s. *(Sony Music)*

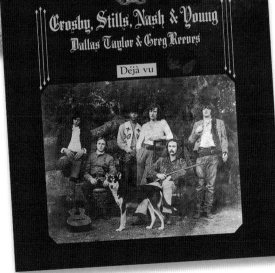

Left: *Sweet Baby James* by James Taylor. After an inauspicious debut album on The Beatles' Apple label, James Taylor delivered the quintessential 70s singer-songwriter record. *(Warner Bros/Warner Music Group)*

Right: *Déjà Vu* by Crosby, Stills, Nash and Young. According to Stephen Stills, 'getting that album out of us was like pulling teeth'. *(Atlantic/Warner Music Group)*

Left: *Benefit* by Jethro Tull. After dabbling with blues and jazz, Ian Anderson moved towards folk-rock – and British 70s prog rock started here. (*Chrysalis/Universal Music Group*)

Right: *Ladies of the Canyon* by Joni Mitchell. Mitchell's sleeve painting included the view from the window of her Laurel Canyon home in her skirt. (*Reprise/Warner Music Group*)

Left: *Let It Be* by The Beatles. The Fab Four's parting shot. Produced by George Martin, shelved for several months, then (said George), 'over-produced by Phil Spector'. (*Apple Corps/Universal Music Group*)

Right: *Live at Leeds* by The Who. How do you follow *Tommy*? With one of the quintessential live albums. 'I didn't think it that good myself' – Roger Daltrey. (*Track/Polydor/ Universal Music Group*)

Left: *Cricklewood Green* by Ten Years After. The record that ensured immortality for one of London's less-heralded locations. (*Deram/Chrysalis/ Universal Music Group*)

Right: *In Rock* by Deep Purple. The American presidents' heads carved 'in rock' on Mount Rushmore inspired one of 1970's most unforgettable sleeve designs. (*Harvest/Universal Music Group*)

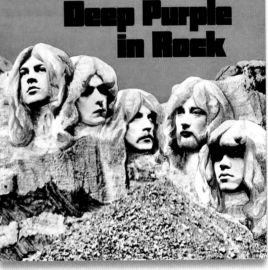

Left: *Full House* by Fairport Convention. Fairport's fifth album was their first without a female vocalist. Now, anyone for cards? (*Island/ Universal Music Group*)

Right: *Mungo Jerry* by Mungo Jerry. Gleeful good-time jug band skiffle and rockabilly, with nods to Elvis and Captain Beefheart and occasional, wistful folk - the blues never sounded so much fun. (*Dawn/ Pye/Warner Music Group*)

Left: *Signed Sealed Delivered* by Stevie Wonder. Stevie's twelfth album, and the first on which he was allowed a greater hand in writing and production. (*Tamla Motown/Universal Music Group*)

Right: *Cosmo's Factory* by Creedence Clearwater Revival. Named after a warehouse in Berkeley, dubbed 'the factory' as leader John Fogerty made them rehearse there nearly every day. (*Fantasy/Concord Music/ Universal Music Group*)

Left: *Get Yer Ya-Yas Out!* By The Rolling Stones. 'Jewels and binoculars hang from the head of the mule' (Dylan, 'Visions of Johanna'), hence the mule beside Charlie Watts. (*Decca/ Universal Music Group*)

Right: *Abraxas* by Santana. As *All Music Guide* says, this eclectic mix of rock, jazz, salsa and blues would later be considered a marketing executive's worst nightmare. (*Sony Music*)

Left: *Atom Heart Mother* by Pink Floyd. The first album to exclude the band's name, photo and title from the main cover, a trend that others soon followed. (*Harvest/Universal Music Group*)

Right: *Led Zeppelin III* by Led Zeppelin. A greater emphasis on acoustic sounds and instruments, and less hard rock, initially surprised some fans and journalists. (*Atlantic/Warner Music Group*)

Left: *Tumbleweed Connection* by Elton John. No singles were released from this Wild West-themed album, but despite that, it remains one of his most acclaimed in retrospect. (*DJM/Rocket/Universal Music Group*)

Right: *Layla and Other Assorted Love Songs* by Derek and the Dominos. Despite featuring Eric Clapton's most-loved seven-minutes, a British commercial failure on release. Who, buyers asked, were Derek and the Dominos? (*Polydor/Universal Music Group*)

Left: *Tea for the Tillerman* by Cat Stevens. Cat followed Joni Mitchell in painting his own sleeve design. The classic track, 'Father and Son', went almost unnoticed at first. (*Island/ Universal Music Group*)

Right: *Lola Versus Powerman and the Money-Go-Round, Part One* by The Kinks. Lola the transvestite, a would-be apeman, and a bitter satire on the music business. It sold badly at home but went Top 40 in the US. (*Pye/ Warner Music Group*)

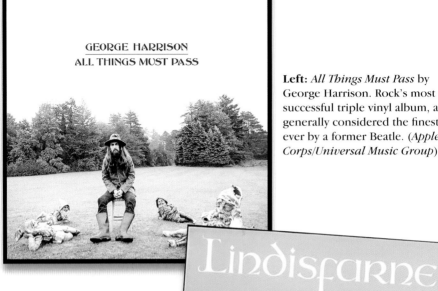

Left: *All Things Must Pass* by George Harrison. Rock's most successful triple vinyl album, and generally considered the finest ever by a former Beatle. (*Apple Corps/Universal Music Group*)

Right: *Nicely Out of Tune* by Lindisfarne. Tyneside's folk-rock Beatles, nicely out of tune with what everyone else was doing at the time. (*Charisma/Universal Music Group*)

Left: *Looking On* by The Move. A neglected prog-rock set combining rock'n'roll riffs, with influences from the classics and jazz, doo-wop. It also marked the birth of ELO. (*Fly/Esoteric/Cherry Red/Proper Music*)

Abraxas – Santana

Personnel:
Carlos Santana: lead guitar, backing vocals
Gregg Rolie: keyboards, lead vocals
David Brown: bass
Michael Shrieve: drums
Jose Pepiro Areas: percussion, congas, timbales
Michael Carabello: percussion, congas
Produced at Wally Heider Studios, San Francisco, and Pacific Recording Studios,
San Mateo, April-May 1970, by Fred Catero, Carlos Santana.
UK release date: November 1970, US release date: September 1970
Record label: CBS, UK; Columbia, US
Highest chart places: UK: 7 US: 1
Running time: 37:10

By the end of the sixties, the San Francisco Bay area had become synonymous
with musical experimentation. In taking much of their inspiration from world
music long before the term became current, mixing it with rock, blues, salsa
and jazz, few groups broke the mould more decisively and made a success
of it than the Latin rock outfit led by guitarist Carlos Santana. They were also
helped by a barnstorming appearance at the Woodstock festival just before the
release of their first album, which received a less than positive reaction from
many American music critics but still charted strongly at number four in the
USA and 26 in the UK. Such success ensured they would be allowed more time
in the studio second time round. It was the follow-up, *Abraxas*, taking its name
from a line in Hermann Hesse's *Demian*, that really put them firmly on the
map. The group were collectively trying to be original. As Santana later noted
in his memoirs, while everybody else was taking ideas from Hendrix and British
musicians, or else R&B players like the Motown session crew, he was thinking
to himself – what was the sound of a soul praying or a ghost crying, and how
could he convey this as a musician?

The album sleeve design was just as bold as the music inside, being based on
Annunciation, a painting from 1961 by German-French artist Mati Klarwein,
who would go on to provide images for album sleeves by Miles Davis, Earth,
Wind & Fire and others.

Santana were an unusual, even unique group. The star of the show was the
lead guitarist who had his roots in the blues, it is true, but at the time, it was
very unusual for half the members to be percussionists. *Abraxas* was one of
those albums that helped to break the mould. In recording an album made
up partly of instrumentals that had no recognisable song structure, it pushed
out the boundaries into a fusion of progressive rock and world music, while
keeping the excitement going and not meandering off into lengthy jams. It
introduced a new genre to a much wider audience in America, Britain and
Europe, something not lost on Anglo-Norwegian group Titanic who reached

the British top five a year later with their cleverly titled instrumental 'Sultana', imitation being the sincerest form of flattery. Maybe it says much that six of the ten tracks on the first of several greatest hits compilations, released in 1974, would be from this album.

'Singing Winds, Crying Beasts' (Michael Carabello)

From the beginning, this promises to be no ordinary rock album. The opening instrumental is not a carefully ordered piece, more a sonic experiment in what can happen when imagination explores the art of the possible. It was the brainchild of Carabello, who sang his ideas to Rolie in preparation for creating a basic percussion track to which Santana could add his contributions. Wafts of shimmering percussion-like wind chimes on a stormy night, stately notes on a Fender Rhodes piano, cymbal effects and then guitar feedback sweeping across from one channel to the other, mesh together while the throb of congas and a simple bass riff act as the background. Taken as a whole, it puts the listener in mind of a faintly menacing soundtrack to a horror movie as it fades into the next track.

'Black Magic Woman/Gypsy Queen' (Peter Green, Gábor Szabó)

Two pieces in one, this begins as a carefully constructed Latin version of the early Fleetwood Mac hit, itself loosely inspired by Otis Rush's 'All Your Love', a 1958 Latin-flavoured blues song. Organ and languid guitar provide a dreamy intro before the main guitar riff leads into the vocal section. Santana had been an admirer of Peter Green's work since seeing Fleetwood Mac live at the Fillmore West and felt the song could be taken further in a slightly different direction. It had some success at home as a single, reaching number four, but not in Britain, where a review in *NME* called it 'exotic and compelling' and 'a positive gem of its kind', but considered it would be of limited appeal. On the album, it segues into an instrumental written by Hungarian jazz guitarist Gábor Szabó, characterised by more Latin percussion and punctuated by ominously stabbing guitar chords and a few seconds of feedback to close.

'Oye Cómo Va' (Tito Puente)

Another tune from the guitarist's youth gets a new treatment in a number that had been a hit a few years earlier for Tito Puente, a bandleader known as the 'King of Latin Music'. Santana liked its infectious dance quality, and he turns the tune – largely instrumental with a few vocal chants – into a feast for jazzy organ, guitar and colourful congas. The result was another successful single, reaching number thirteen in the US.

'Incident at Neshabur' (Alberto Gianquinto, Carlos Santana)

The album's second instrumental was co-written by Gianquinto, a jazz pianist and friend of Santana. Full of light and shade, the bustling congas, organ phrases and guitar riffs usher in a tune that is characterised by the contrast between Giaquinto's more conventional jazzy style, and Rolie's other keyboards, both organ and Fender Rhodes, with the rhythms ever-changing. Just over halfway through a more restrained passage begins as guitar phrases curl around the smooth organ notes and piano patterns. At one point, it almost stops altogether and floats gently downstream to a graceful finish. As Rolie later commented, this was one of his favourites as they did not consciously know what they were doing when they started but simply 'did time changes, colours, and things that musically were very sophisticated'.

'Se a Cabó' (José Areas)
One of the instrumentals by percussionist Areas that bookended side two is partly a showcase for his congas and timbales. An insistent bassline and short sharp bursts of guitar also help to set the mood, incorporating a punchy guitar solo further on. At less than three minutes, this is short and sweet, but like the other instrumentals, improvisation ensured that when they played live on stage, these numbers branched out into much greater length.

'Mother's Daughter' (Gregg Rolie)
Having come through more of a conventional hard rock apprenticeship, Rolie would later leave Santana to help form Journey. The first of his two songs on the album is something of a departure from the previous numbers and almost sounds like a different group altogether. With a lyric about a cheating woman whose 'stupid game is about to end', a heavy R'n'B riff (with shades of The Spencer Davos Group's evergreen 'Gimme Some Lovin'') is punctuated by several flashes of lightning on organ and guitar, as the soulful vocals work themselves up into a frenzy.

'Samba Pa Ti' (Santana)
Here is the instrumental that went on to achieve more or less classic status. Santana said it was inspired by listening to a drunken street musician playing jazz on the saxophone outside his New York apartment one Sunday afternoon but at times seemed unable to decide whether he should be putting the bottle or saxophone to his mouth first. A melody came to the guitarist at once, feeling it was the first song that he felt really belonged to him, the first true representation of 'my tone, my fingerprints, my identity, my uniqueness'. (Should the busker have been asked his name and given a joint credit?) Almost five minutes long, the guitar flows almost effortlessly as organ and percussion slowly build from about halfway through. Several other artists would later cover the piece, among them José Feliciano, who provided lyrics. In the mid-1970s, it was released as a single to promote a greatest hits collection and never charted in America though becoming a hit in several European countries (including number 27 in the UK). In Britain, it became for a time an enduring favourite in discos as 'the last smooch' record of the evening.

'Hope You're Feeling Better' (Rolie)

This is the closest the album gets to hard rock and also a sense of fun. Like his previous song, despite the Latin percussion fills, it has quite a different character from the other seven tracks. Despite what the guitarist may have said to the contrary, there seems to be more than a hint of Hendrix in the incendiary, even psychedelic soloing and wah-wah work that come towards the end.

'El Nicoya' (Areas)

The second contribution from Areas is basically a percussion jam, with guitar relegated to the background for a change and the title chanted at intervals. At only 90 seconds long, it is little more than a bookend, but a good way to finish.

Atom Heart Mother – Pink Floyd

Personnel:
Roger Waters: bass, classical guitar, lead vocals, tape effects, tape collages
David Gilmour: guitars, bass, drums, percussion, lead vocals
Richard Wright: Hammond organ, piano, Farfisa organ, mellotron
Nick Mason: drums, percussion
EMI Pops Orchestra: brass and orchestral sections
Ron Geesin: orchestrations
Haflidi Hallgrimson: cello
John Alldis Choir: vocals
Alan Styles: voice and sound effects
Peter Bown: engineering
Alan Parsons: engineering
Nick Mason: tape effects, tape collages
Recorded at Abbey Road, London, March-August 1970
Produced by Pink Floyd and Norman Smith.
UK release date: October 1970
US release date: October 1970
Record label: Harvest
Highest chart places: UK: 1 US: 55
Running time: 52:06

Pink Floyd's fifth studio album, their first British No. 1, and the first on EMI's new progressive and rock label Harvest to reach the top, was also the group's first not to feature their name on the sleeve, or contain any photographs of the group, something they would follow throughout the rest of their career.

All in all, *Atom Heart Mother* is a strange album. The first side is a remarkable fusion of instrumental sounds, comparable to what The Nice and Deep Purple were doing at the same time by bringing or writing classical music and integrating it into conventional rock instrumentation. The three songs stand up well on their own, but the finale might be a case of 'the emperor's new clothes'.

In allowing an extended suite to take up one side of an album, it was perhaps the godfather of Mike Oldfield's extended compositions on *Tubular Bells* and others. There was a marked difference in that Oldfield was almost a one-man band in the studio, writing and arranging everything and relying little on outside musicians or ensembles, to play what went down on tape. Moreover, his compositions tended to be more accessible and melodic, even more commercial, drawing from folk traditions as well as more conventional rock, ambient and modern classical ideas. Pink Floyd were breaking new ground, and for a record that was determined to go against the grain and be anything but a batch of radio-friendly songs, even though they had long had and held on to their faithful fan base, it proved remarkably successful. To this day, in polls of 'Floyd albums ranked from best to worst,' it generally achieves around seventh or eighth place.

Atom Heart Mother (Nick Mason – David Gilmour – Roger Waters – Richard Wright – Ron Geesin): **I. Father's Shout** (Gilmour, Geesin) – **II. Breast Milky** (Wright – Gilmour – Geesin – Mason) – **III. Mother Fore** (Gilmour – Wright – Geesin) – **IV. Funky Dung** (Wright – Waters – Gilmour) – **V. Mind Your Throats Please** (Wright – Gilmour – Mason – Waters) – **VI. Remergence** (Gilmour – Geesin – Wright)

The entire first side is taken up by the title track, a suite in six parts lasting almost 24 minutes, entirely instrumental apart from two shouts close to the end. It was developed from instrumental ideas they had composed during recent rehearsals and brought together into a more coherent unit. When they were required to use new state-of-the-art technical equipment recently added at Abbey Road Studios, they were told they could not do any tape splicing to edit different pieces together. Waters on bass and Mason on drums, therefore, had to play the full piece in one sitting, with the other two overdubbing their contributions at a later stage.

After completing the track, they felt it lacked something. Enter composer and musician Ron Geesin, who they felt would be the right person to compose an orchestral arrangement to be laid over their backing tracks. Unlike The Beatles (well, three of them) who had wanted strings, brass and backing vocals added to *Let It Be*, Floyd went the opposite route. They needed the enhancements – and the music written as well – to take centre stage while they were in effect the backing group, then went on an American tour while Geesin set to work. Gilmour supplied some of the melodic lines, while he and Wright jointly supervised the middle section featuring the sixteen-piece choir, conducted by John Alldis as he had more experience than Geesin.

This extended suite, which had working titles of 'Untitled Epic' on Geesin's score, and then 'The Amazing Pudding', was played at Bath Festival at the end of May. For a BBC Radio 1 *In Concert* broadcast in mid-July, it needed a proper name so John Peel could introduce it, and 'Atom Heart Mother', from a newspaper headline, was chosen by Waters. It is split loosely into six sections, but vinyl and most CD pressings treat it as a whole and do not sub-divide it.

'Father's Shout' opens portentously with Hammond organ and brass, like a slow march or theme music to a suspense film of the period. The group then enter, but the brass remains dominant, and the theme is reprised several times.

'Breast Milky' is for much of the way a sweet organ part, plus cello solo and bass, later joined by drums and slide guitar, and choir at the end.

'Mother Fore' is mainly choral, the organ plus muted bass and drums, joined by soprano voices and then the choir, swelling to a dramatic crescendo and dying down at the end.

'Funky Dung' is basically a group jam session with grand piano and Farfisa organ to the fore, plus a bluesy guitar solo and the choir providing a chanting section. At the end comes a reprise of the main theme from 'Father's Shout'.

'Mind Your Throats Please' sees the introduction of electronic noises, mellotron, the distorted 'Here is a loud announcement!' and the sound of a passing steam train. Instruments fade in and out, some recognisable from having been heard earlier in the suite, plus piano, brass, a shout of 'Silence in the studio!' and some discordant sound collages towards the end.

'Remergence', the closing section, starts with a reprise of the 'Father's Shout' theme, followed by organ and the cello solo, followed by a double layered guitar section reminiscent of the first slide solo. This leads into a climactic final reprise of the 'Father's Shout' theme with the entire brass section and choir, ending with a coda from the choir and brass. Throughout, the music has its share of alternating passages from choral vocals, brass and strings, which hark back to a classical tradition, interspersed with the more obvious guitar-bass-drums sections alongside the more nightmarish sound effects. Floyd had experimented with similar left-field styles already, but this time they took a leap forward, admittedly with more experienced collaborators on board.

'If' (Waters)

Side two presents three more conventional tracks and another adventure. The first is mainly the work of Waters, a largely acoustic ballad on which he plays acoustic guitar, with soft organ and bass in the background. It is an introspective number, partly inspired by Rudyard Kipling's poem of the same title, and listening to it brings visions to mind a solo folksinger playing as he sits in the countryside. With lines like 'If I go insane, please don't put your wires in my brain', it hints at some of the darker themes that would be explored in depth in the group's subsequent work.

'Summer '68' (Wright)

A more lively affair, an invigorating number that tells in veiled terms of an encounter with a groupie a couple of years earlier. It was issued as a single in Japan, and is clearly the most commercial four minutes on the whole album. With its cheerful piano, acoustic guitars and lively brass section hinting at a fairground atmosphere, this is psychedelic pop that might not have sounded out of place on The Beatles' *Sergeant Pepper*. It is certainly the only part of the record that could be described as radio-friendly.

'Fat Old Sun' (Gilmour)

Another slow, wistful number backed mostly by acoustic guitar and organ, this has shades of some of the material Ray Davies was writing for The Kinks' *Village Green Preservation Society* album. There is a decidedly pastoral flavour to the music and to lines describing 'the sound of music in my ears, distant bells, new-mown grass smells so sweet, by the river holding hands'. It builds up to a powerful guitar solo, cross-fading with the sound of church bells in the distance. During his subsequent solo career, it would have a regular place in Gilmour's live show, often ending in a lengthy jam.

Alan's Psychedelic Breakfast (Waters – Mason – Gilmour – Wright): I. Rise and Shine – II. Sunny Side Up – III. Morning Glory

After a return to normality, the grand finale is twelve minutes, divided into three parts; or should that be courses? Depending on your point of view – and critics, both at the time and also retrospectively, have been split down the middle – this is either a case of 'weird but innovative, somehow it works', or 'what on earth were they thinking of when they did THIS?' Although credited to all four, it evolved mainly through Waters experimenting with the rhythm of a dripping tap, which was combined with sound effects and dialogue recorded by Mason in his kitchen, plus musical effects recorded at Abbey Road. Alan Styles was then the group's roadie, and this is the sound of him preparing, discussing and eating his breakfast, while the group play in the background. He mutters to himself about 'macrobiotic stuff', scrambled eggs, sausages and coffee, to the accompaniment of pouring out a bowl of cereal (complete with snap, crackle and pop), lighting the stove, cooking bacon, drinking, gulping down food, and then a kettle whistling. Gilmour then plays a piece on two acoustic guitars and steel guitar, punctuated by the dripping tap and the sound of someone washing up. The last part is largely keyboards, Wright's piano and Hammond organ, plus guitar, bass, and drums. Piano brings the music to a finish, someone lets the water out of the sink, Alan admits that 'my head's a blank', picks up the car keys, and the faint sound of a car is heard driving away. On the vinyl version, the dripping tap at the end is cut into the run-off groove and plays on until the stylus is lifted off. On paper, it is an interesting, even original idea, but perhaps something only the really hardened fan would want to listen to more than occasionally.

Led Zeppelin III – Led Zeppelin

Personnel:
Robert Plant: vocals
Jimmy Page: guitars, pedal steel guitar, banjo, backing vocal, bass
John Paul Jones: bass, Hammond organ, synthesiser, mandolin, double bass
John Bonham: drums
Produced at Rolling Stones Mobile Studio, Hedley Grange, Hampshire; Island
Studios, and Olympic Studios, London, May-August 1970, by Jimmy Page.
UK and US release date: October 1970
Record label: Atlantic
Highest chart places: UK: 1, US: 1
Running time: 43:04

Most of Led Zeppelin's third album was written by Robert Plant and Jimmy
Page while they were staying at Bron-Y-Aur, a cottage in rural Wales. The
environment gave them a chance to come up with songs that demonstrated
a greater emphasis on folk and acoustic sounds. Although they had always
included one or two songs in this direction, this more restrained collection
came as something of a shock to fans expecting mostly more variations on
'Whole Lotta Love'.

The record met with a lukewarm critical reception and more modest sales,
notwithstanding its status as the first of their albums to enter the charts at
pole position. 'Led Zeppelin go acoustic' was the response of some baffled
critics, and Page was so irritated by the reaction that he refused to give any
more interviews to the press for over a year. Nevertheless, its reputation has
since soared, as an innovative set that was not content to retread past glories
and saw them covering new musical ground. While it included a couple of
tracks that pleased those expecting more guitar riffs, scorching solos and
Plant's inimitable scream, it also had a generous nod to the vintage blues
pioneers who had inspired them in the first place, as well as the unashamed
experimentation with different sounds and instruments.

'Immigrant Song' (Page, Plant)
Track one was a joy to those who loved their heroes hard and heavy. Plant's
lyrics to 'Immigrant Song' had been inspired by a recent visit to Iceland,
which conjured up images of Vikings and large ships. A maelstrom of guitar,
bass and drums in unison powers the song throughout, with a couple of
brief stops and restarts along the way. At just over two minutes in length,
there is no space for any soloing, just a relentless wall of sound as he sings
at full throttle of men in earlier times whose 'only goal will be the western
shore', urged on by the cry of 'Valhalla, I am coming!' Released as a single in
America, it reached No. 16.

'Friends' (Page, Plant)

This is where the group's long-lasting fascination with Eastern-influenced music began, and it is one of their few songs to include strings, arranged by Jones. The combined effect of open tuning on Page's guitar and Bonham's tabla drums help to evoke the sound of Indian classical music to lyrics in which Plant sings of bonhomie towards one's fellow man. Quite a radical departure from their usual sound, it has overtones of groups like Crosby, Stills, Nash & Young.

'Celebration Day' (John Paul Jones, Page, Plant)

Inspired by one of Plant's visits to New York City, this is almost a return to high-voltage rock with a smattering of funk. It flows from the previous track with a frenzied intro of guitar chords, played at high speed on top of a monotonic drone from a synthesiser. The specific meaning of the lyrics has sparked much debate, with some believing the woman referred to is a groupie, others that she might be an oppressed woman of colour fighting for equal rights.

'Since I've Been Loving You' (Jones, Page, Plant)

The album's main excursion into blues territory is also the longest track at over seven minutes. Similar to some of the material on their first album, it is a slow, moody piece coloured throughout by Hammond organ, with Page's solo and Plant's controlled whisper-to-a-scream providing plenty of light and shade.

'Out on the Tiles' (John Bonham, Page, Plant)

One of the hard-drinking Bonham's favourite expressions inspired Plant to write a lyric around the title, hence his inclusion in the writing credit. Nevertheless, it became more or less a love song, the title being absent from the lyrics, including a guitar riff that Page worked up from a jamming session. It is one of the album's least interesting moments, with the last half of the four minutes features the same guitar and pattern, with Plant's 'ooh yeah' repeated ad infinitum until the fade.

'Gallows Pole' (traditional, arranged Page, Plant)

The origins of this can be traced back to an old 1930s song by Leadbelly, if not further, to an old traditional number about a woman who tries to bribe the hangman and escape execution. From a fairly relaxed tempo at the beginning, it gradually speeds up, particularly when the drums come in about two minutes later. Page plays several acoustic and electric guitars as well as banjo, while Jones adds mandolin.

'Tangerine' (Page, Plant)

Folk Zeppelin present an uncharacteristically pretty song about lost love, rather in the vein of Donovan (for whom Page and Jones had played several sessions in earlier days) or Neil Young. It opens with a few seconds of delicately picked guitar, stops, and begins again after a brief count-in. Again, Page plays several guitars acoustic, electric and pedal steel, while Jones adds mandolin as well as bass. Plant's vocal is double-tracked as he harmonises with himself, and Bonham's drums do not come in until about a minute after the start, and later pausing for effect. The pastoral mood of this song suggests something of a dress rehearsal for 'Stairway To Heaven' on the next album.

'That's the Way' (Page, Plant)

Social concerns are addressed in what is probably their most thought-provoking lyric yet. Written by Plant and Page after returning from a long walk in the countryside, it reflected the former's views on the environment and ecology, hence the mention of fish dying in dirty waters, and flowers by the roadside – 'all that lives is born to die'. There are also veiled references to how the group had been treated in America during the initial tours when they were spat on, had guns drawn at them, and were heckled at airports and on planes because of their long hair, and on their concerns about the violence they had seen policemen use against protesters against the Vietnam war, and on fans at their shows. More pedal steel guitar, mandolin and even dulcimer are used to good effect on one of their most melodic numbers yet.

'Bron-Y-Aur Stomp' (Jones, Page, Plant)

The last two tracks show a pronounced move into acoustic territory. This is a cheery four minutes of jug band skiffle, closer to Lonnie Donegan or Mungo Jerry. Named after the cottage where Plant and Page had been staying, it means 'hillside of gold' in Welsh. Plant sings a carefree celebration of walking down leafy country lanes with just a dog for company, accompanied by Page on acoustic guitar, Jones's stand-up double bass, and Bonham's spoons and castanets.

'Hats Off to (Roy) Harper' (Traditional, arranged Charles Obscure)

'Charles Obscure' was an alias used by Page, who based it largely on Bukka White's old blues song 'Shake 'Em On Down', on what was probably the strangest track they ever recorded. The lyrics are freely adapted from various numbers by the likes of Robert Johnson, Arthur Crudup and Sleepy John Estes as well as White, and they had sometimes included snatches of these songs in medleys on stage while jamming spontaneously on 'Whole Lotta Love' and others. Page plays bottleneck guitar, while Plant sings through a vibrato amp, giving a deliberately distorted effect to simulate an old vintage blues record remastered from a 78 r.p.m. disc – if it was not for the fact that guitar comes mainly from one stereo channel and vocals from the other. Jones and Bonham are nowhere to be heard. To some listeners, it sounds like an unintelligible mess, a half-baked concoction of guitar chords and annoying vocals that badly need polishing. As for the lyrics, they have a tenuous connection with Roy Harper, the contemporary folk singer whom they had befriended when both acts were on the bill at the Bath Festival that summer. When he visited the group's Oxford Street office one day, Page gave him a copy of the album, urged him to look at the print more closely – and he was astonished to see his name in the title of the last track. Page explained the title by saying that he took his hat off to anybody who does what they think is right and refuses to sell out.

Tumbleweed Connection – Elton John

Personnel:
Elton John: lead and backing vocals, piano, Hammond organ
Brian Dee: Hammond organ
Caleb Quaye: lead and acoustic guitars
Les Thatcher: acoustic guitar
Gordon Huntley: steel guitar
Lesley Duncan: backing vocals, acoustic guitar
Mike Egan: acoustic guitar
Dave Glover, Herbie Flowers: bass
Chris Laurence: acoustic bass
Dee Murray: backing vocals, bass
Roger Pope, Barry Morgan: drums, percussion
Nigel Olsson: backing vocals, drums
Robin Jones: congas, tambourine
Karl Jenkins: oboe
Skaila Kanga: harp
Ian Duck: harmonica
Johnny Van Derrick: violin
Madeline Bell, Tony Burrows, Kay Garner, Tony Hazzard, Dusty Springfield,
Tammi Hunt, Heather Wheatman, Yvonne Wheatman: backing vocals
Produced at Trident Studios, London, March 1970, by Gus Dudgeon.
UK release date: October 1970; US release date: January 1971
Record label: DJM, UK; Uni, US.
Highest chart places: UK: 2, US: 5
Running time: 46:56
All songs written by Elton John and Bernie Taupin, unless stated otherwise.

Elton John's third album, and his second to be released in 1970, was unique in that it charted very highly and sold well, despite no singles being released from it in Britain, Europe or America. It was loosely a concept album about the American West, even though neither John nor his lyricist Bernie Taupin had ever set foot on the other side of the Atlantic until after it was written. The songs dealt with civil war imagery, references to farmyards, swallows, gunslingers, saloons and one-horse towns, an atmosphere enhanced by the sepia imagery on the front and back of the gatefold sleeve, ironically based on a photo taken at Sheffield Park Station, Sussex. Taupin admitted that it had a theme in a down-home way, being heavily influenced like so many other musicians at the time by The Band's first two albums.

By John's standards, none of these ten songs are particularly well known and have rarely appeared on compilations or even been hits for other artists. Nevertheless, at a time when he was remarkably prolific, over fifty years later, the album is still regarded as one of his best ever. Several recent internet 'albums ranked worst to best' polls from *Rolling Stone*, *Classic Rock* and others have placed it in his top three, one even at the top.

'Ballad of a Well-Known Gun'
Lyrically and musically, this outlaw narrative in song sets the tone well for the whole album. It sounds less like the former Pinner pub pianist, more like something that The Band or Leon Russell might have written and recorded, or even the countrified Rolling Stones with Mick Jagger out front perfecting his best mock-cowboy drawl. Caleb Quaye's unobtrusive but funky guitar phrases complement the piano work well with a hint of New Orleans-style swing, while there is a marvellous touch of call-and-respond towards the end as Dusty Springfield and Madeline Bell sing 'There goes the well-known gun', with John answering 'Now they've found me.'

'Come Down in Time'
Almost a genuine folk ballad, or even in lullaby territory as the record continues. With its soothing acoustic guitar and bass, harp and oboe, and the lightest touch imaginable from Paul Buckmaster's string arrangement, the lyrics portray a tender mood of peace, quiet, only the half-light of a moon, 'while a cluster of nightjars sang some songs out of tune'.

'Country Comfort'
Sometimes one comes across a track where everything simply falls into place. An utterly infectious chorus, masterful tune throughout, a rich musical tapestry with steel guitar, harmonica and fiddle, all adding touches in the background, are all compelling enough even before we reach the lyrics. Here are the pleasures of small-town life – heartwarming little vignettes of village children having a scrap, pines falling everywhere, the local deacon preparing his next sermon, an octogenarian grandma asking for a hand to fix her barn, while right at the end comes the evocative picture, 'Across the valley moves the herdsman with his torch'. It was also covered by Rod Stewart, Kate Taylor (James's sister), and some years later by Keith Urban.

'Son of Your Father'
Another of those songs that might almost have been written by The Band, lyrically, it is a dark tale of an argument between an elderly farmer who has a hook for a hand and someone who owes him money. By the end of the song, both men are lying dead. Despite the grim subject matter, it is a lively tune, driven by infectious backing vocals on the chorus, a full-blooded brass arrangement, plus some funky guitar and harmonica throughout. The song had already been offered to Spooky Tooth and recorded as a single the previous year.

110

'My Father's Gun'
In the six-minute epic that closes side one, another downbeat number tells of a young Confederate soldier whose father has been killed in battle during the American Civil War. After laying him to rest, the young man takes possession of his weapon so he can join the fighting and the cause his father fought for, as well as avenge his death. As he sails on the riverboat to an uncertain future, he dreams of a happy ending in that one day he will return, in victory and peace, to his lands and family. A slow, stately number, it gathers momentum with the gospel backing vocals plus a stately arrangement on strings and horns.

'Where To Now St Peter?'
Once more, a soldier has died in battle – during the Civil War, it is assumed – and is passing over to the hereafter. The general theme has some similarities with the World War One poem by Wilfred Owen's World War One poem *Strange Meeting*, in which a comrade in arms meets the foe who slew him on the western front. He is about to find out where his fate lies for posterity, as the title suggests, singing, 'I may not be a Christian, but I've done all one man can'. Quaye shines forth with some intriguing wah-wah work, plus some nifty acoustic guitar and subtle drumming.

'Love Song' (Lesley Duncan)
The only number that John and Taupin did not write, sounds completely out of character on the album and rather breaks the flow of the concept. Sung as a duet with its writer to the folksy accompaniment of an acoustic guitar, it makes pleasant enough listening but is nothing special. There is, however, an attractive simplicity to it in that it could have been drenched in strings and sounded rather bland as a result. What does sound a little distracting is the last thirty seconds or so, which sound like waves on the seashore with children playing.

'Amoreena'
The second love song in a row is more complex and rather more interesting than the first. The lyrics dwell on the lady that the singer misses, as he recalls carefree days of a girl playing freely in the cornfield, 'living like a lusty flower, running through the grass for hours, rolling through the hay'. Musically it is mid-tempo, marking the debut of the rhythm section of Nigel Olsson on drums and Dee Murray on bass, Elton John regulars for the next few years, behind the piano and organ that recall Al Kooper's playing on mid-1960s Dylan sessions. Amoreena was the name subsequently given to the daughter of Ray Williams, who was John and Taupin's manager at the time when his wife was expecting a child. The association ended shortly afterwards in acrimony following a dispute with their music publisher, Dick James. However, the song would live on, when used during the opening credits of the Sidney Lumet and Al Pacino picture *Dog Day Afternoon*.

'Talking Old Soldiers'

This song is simplicity itself – it's just John, his voice and piano, with no strings, no echo, and even no vocal backing. Alternately welcoming, sad, even a little angry, he seats himself in the saloon bar as he offers to buy his old comrade in arms another beer. It may be somewhat short on melody but makes up for it in passion, as he (or should we say Taupin) ponders what it is like to grow old, remembering when he could drink three times as much as he can now, as he passed the time away with old friends at the same bar who have since passed away. He has seen enough to make a man go out of his mind, he contemplates; 'do they know what it's like to have a graveyard as a friend?' It may be gloomy, even depressing, but even so, it is perhaps the most moving lyric on the whole album. The thought occurs that the addition of a brass or jazz band, even sparingly, might have underscored the melancholy more poignantly, but then sometimes more is less, and less is more.

'Burn Down the Mission'

The grand finale – and the record's masterstroke – comes with what has long been heralded as one of the very best songs from John's first three or four albums. The subject matter, we assume, is a Christian mission, and the temptation of a starving man driven to torch the building as it contains enough food to feed him and many others. His wife cried when they came to take him away, he sings with anger, but what more could he do to keep her warm than burn down the mission walls? Another ballad in the most downbeat hue of sepia, you might think at first, as he accompanies himself at the ivories again for the first few seconds. Then he hits the higher notes as organ, acoustic guitar and rhythm section join in – then he goes up, up, up with that chorus. Two minutes in, it takes an apocalyptic turn and sounds like another song for all of thirty seconds, with a simple but distinctive pattern of piano chords, drums and brass surge behind. Everything falls quiet for the next verse and chorus, until three minutes later, it returns to the big, bold tempo change and that intense interplay spearheaded by piano and brass. All we are missing is one massive bombastic ending instead of the fade. It became one of the centrepieces of his stage show over the years. An in-concert broadcast on American radio that subsequently became his first live album, *17-11-70* (named after the date it went out) in order to pre-empt the bootleggers, closed with a tour de force version lasing about fifteen minutes, interpolating a rock'n'roll medley of 'My Baby Left Me' and 'Get Back'.

Layla and Other Assorted Love Songs – Derek and the Dominos

Personnel:
Eric Clapton: vocals, guitars
Bobby Whitlock: vocals, keyboards, acoustic guitar
Carl Radle: bass, percussion
Jim Gordon: drums, percussion, piano
Duane Allman: slide guitars
Albhy Galuten: piano
Produced at Criteria Studios, Miami, August-October 1970, by Tom Dowd, Derek and the Dominos.
UK release date: December 1970, US release date: November 1970
Record label: Polydor, UK: Atco, US
Highest chart places: UK: 68 (in 2011), US: 16
Running time: 76:44

Longing to escape the universal 'Clapton is God' adulation, consumed by his romantic passion for Patti (Mrs George Harrison) and drug problems, Clapton was intent on submerging his identity with a group not made up of two or three major names. Derek and the Dominos was the result, formed after he had written several songs with Whitlock, then teamed up with the rhythm section of Radle and Gordon. All three had been part of Delaney & Bonnie and Friends, a group with whom Clapton had played and jammed on an informal basis. Their producer Tom Dowd had been working on an Allman Brothers album. Clapton and Duane Allman immediately started jamming together, and the latter accordingly ended up playing on all but the first three tracks on the ensuing album.

Although it has generally been tagged as a blues album, there is a remarkably eclectic mix on display. This is no collection of variations on the much-tried and tested 12-bar blues theme, but a vibrant collection of songs with two guitar geniuses, Clapton and Allman, bouncing off each other, backed by other musicians who sound as if they are having the time of their lives. The strangest factor of all is that, with hindsight, we know there were so many dubious substances being freely used that it is astonishing they managed to complete over seventy minutes' worth of such marvellous music to such high quality in a very short space of time. Above all, Clapton, who had never been the primary vocalist in Cream and Blind Faith, and merely the guitarist before that with John Mayall's Bluesbreakers and The Yardbirds, had been encouraged to sing his heart out with a passion – and acquits himself with a feeling and consistency he never achieved before and in several decades of solo albums has rarely done since.

The album did not chart in Britain on release, partly because (despite promotional badges saying 'Derek is Eric') many buyers were unaware that

113

this was Eric Clapton and his band, and perhaps as there had been a recent glut of albums from him at the time, with Cream, Blind Faith sets, and a solo collection not long before. A CD release in 2011 gave it one week of glory. It received a very critical attention on its first appearance, and only with hindsight has it been revaluated as his genuine masterpiece in a career spanning over half a century.

'I Looked Away' (Eric Clapton, Bobby Whitlock)

An infectious song set to a shuffling country beat with both guitars playing in lively style against each other, the lyrics set the tone for a mood that pervades much of the album. It hints at an illicit affair between a man and a woman who knows he is sinning by loving the wife of another. She persuades him that she will always be there and never walk away from him, but once he looks away, she leaves. In spite of that, he will keep on sinning for the rest of his life. Whitlock adds vocal harmonies and sings a verse about halfway through. Michael Nesmith covered it a year later.

'Bell Bottom Blues' (Clapton, Whitlock)

In a record stacked with the goods, the lovelorn 'Bell Bottom Blues' is generally seen as one of the outstanding tracks. The lyrics are said to be about a girl whom Clapton had briefly known in France who wore bell-bottomed trousers, and with whom he was infatuated for a while. Sweetly melodic blues guitar and organ lines punctuate vocals laden with emotion, the outpourings of a love affair that can never be, as he asks the object of his affections if she wants to see him crawl across the floor to her as he begs her to take me back. 'I don't want to fade away, give me one more day.'

'Keep On Growing' (Clapton, Whitlock)

Initially, an instrumental jam called 'Airport Shuffle', this was going to be discarded. Whitlock thought it was far too good to waste, so he wrote a melody and lyrics on the theme of 'a young man and sure to go astray' until the right girl walks into his life and tells him love will find a way'. When he tried to sing it himself, he was dissatisfied, but everyone else loved the song, so he suggested to Clapton that they should do 'a Sam & Dave thing – you sing a line, I sing a line, we'll sing a line together'. With its shared vocals, shuffling rhythm and dual guitars, it is another of the record's highlights. Towards the end, Whitlock spontaneously delivers a couple of bars on organ in another rhythm, as if about to begin a different song altogether.

'Nobody Knows You When You're Down and Out' (Jimmy Cox)

The oldest song here was originally a roaring twenties anthem written by Jimmy Cox in 1923. Moody, mournful blues in which the singer reflects on having lived the life of a millionaire during the prohibition era and then fallen on hard times, Clapton imbues the lines with anguish and despair while bleeding notes pour forth from the guitar and gently shimmering organ.

'I Am Yours' (Clapton, Nizami)
The first of two songs on the album inspired by 'The Story of Layla and Majnun' by 12th-century Persian poet Nizami, has Clapton setting some of his text to music. Basically, a gentle bossa nova tune with Gordon adding a soft shuffle on the bongos, it makes an inoffensive if rather unexceptional love song.

'Anyday' (Clapton, Whitlock)
This is another number with a message of how good love could be if only both partners could sink their differences: 'someday baby, I know you're gonna need me when this whole world has got you down.' Clapton and Whitlock take turns on providing lead vocal on the verses with a soulful intensity against a funky rhythm, while Allman's slide guitar shines throughout.

'Key to the Highway' (Charlie Segar, Willie Broonzy)
The album's longest track was a happy accident. When Clapton and Allman heard Domingo Samudio (Sam the Sham of 'Wooly Bully' fame) recording the song in a neighbouring studio, they immediately decided to play it themselves. Tom Dowd heard them and told the engineers to hit the record button at once. Originally written around 1940 and recorded by many blues artists since then, in the group's hands, this mid-tempo number is a sheer delight, a jam with occasional vocals that in almost ten minutes never flags.

'Tell the Truth' (Clapton, Whitlock)
The first song the then four-strong group recorded was laid down in London in June, with Harrison and Dave Mason also on guitars, shortly after they had all been working on Harrison's *All Things Must Pass*. Played at a faster pace and only three minutes long, Phil Spector produced it and it was briefly released as a single in America in September, before they ordered it to be withdrawn. The album version from the Dowd-produced sessions, without the two British guitarists but with Allman, was about twice as long and rather slower. Most of it had been Whitlock's work, with Clapton adding the last verse. Once again, both writers shared vocals on alternate verses. Whereas the original is almost rockabilly in style, this has more of a Rolling Stones feel, with Allman's slide guitar adding particular punch.

'Why Does Love Got To Be So Sad?' (Clapton, Whitlock)
Although the downbeat title might suggest otherwise, this is played at breakneck pace, with the entire group on fire. All the guitarists are fairly bouncing off each other in the jam session after the vocals end, although the rhythm section eventually pauses for breath and it glides to a calm conclusion.

'Have You Ever Loved a Woman?' (Billy Myles)
Clapton had loved this blues song ever since hearing the Freddie King version, and first recorded it while playing with John Mayall around 1965. A slow, stately number, once again, it proves an ideal showcase for both guitarists.

'Little Wing' (Jimi Hendrix)
Always one of Clapton's favourite Hendrix songs, he thought it was much more structured and melodic than most of his other work, and enjoyed the lyrical images of 'a child walking through the clouds with a circus mind that's running wild'. They recorded their version out of admiration to a living legend, ironically just a few days before Hendrix died.

'It's Too Late' (Chuck Willis)
A hit for Chuck Willis is 1956 comes in the shape of a gently rolling blues, similar in pace to 'The Great Pretender'. Another one to feature the Clapton-Whitlock call-and-response routine, it was the only song the group ever performed on television when they appeared one night on *The Johnny Cash Show*.

'Layla' (Clapton, Jim Gordon)
Clapton originally wrote a ballad, inspired by his love for Pattie Harrison, a celebration in song about which she was not very happy. Its roots were in Nizami's 'Layla and Majnun', about a man in love with a woman but cannot have her because her parents object, and when they are torn apart, he goes mad. It became faster when Allman added the song's main guitar riff, based on the one from Albert King's 'As the Years Go Passing By'. When Clapton heard Gordon playing a section on piano that he claimed was his own work (although lifted from a tune his ex-girlfriend Rita Coolidge had written), Clapton asked to have it added to the song as a coda. Gordon received a co-credit, but Coolidge, Allman and King did not. Despite being a collage of other peoples' work, 'Layla' was soon acclaimed as a rock classic. An edited version faded before the piano part was issued as a single in 1972 to promote a compilation album, and reached No.7 in Britain, and then No. 4 again ten years later.

'Thorn Tree in the Garden' (Whitlock)
The album comes to an end on what is largely a Whitlock solo piece that he had written about a neighbour with whom he had an argument, hence the title. At less than three minutes, it was the shortest track of all, and they recorded it acoustically, all gathered around a single microphone.

Tea For The Tillerman – Cat Stevens

Personnel:
Cat Stevens: classical guitar, acoustic guitar, keyboards, vibraphone, lead vocals
Alun Davies: acoustic guitar, backing vocals
Harvey Burns: drums, congas, tambourine
John Ryan: double bass
John Rostein: violin
Produced at Morgan Studios, Island Studios, Olympic Studios, all London, May-July 1970, by Paul Samwell-Smith.
UK release date: December 1970, US release date: January 1971
Record label: Island, UK: A&M, US
Highest chart places: UK: 20, US: 8
Running time: 36:49
All songs written by Cat Stevens.

The newly-reborn, fully recovered folk singer-songwriter Cat Stevens was remarkably prolific in 1970. During his illness and convalescence, he had written several songs that he could not wait to record, resulting in two albums at seven-month intervals. The first, *Mona Bone Jakon*, was a rather downbeat set. This was the more confident, albeit often questioning, and more instantly successful follow-up. Though it was not intended as a concept album, most of the songs followed along the twin themes of conflict between the generations, and also spiritual meaning religion as an indirect answer to the questions of contemporary life and society.

'Where Do the Children Play?'
While Joni Mitchell was alerting music listeners to environmental concerns in America, Cat Stevens was doing likewise on the other side of the Atlantic. As a youngster in London, his playground had been a basement rather than green spaces with open air. As a young adult, he looked at the world around him, the ever-accelerating technological advances, jumbo planes, rolling on roads over fresh green grass for lorry loads pumping petrol gas, and skyscrapers reaching ever higher. For the first two verses and choruses, his acoustic guitar is the main accompaniment, until an electric piano and backing vocals take their bow. In the last verse, his voice rises a notch with sheer passion, aided by a steady beat on the drums and Del Newman's discreet but effective strings. Like Mitchell, he was quite ahead of his time, but his message has become ever more relevant in the years since it first appeared.

'Hard Headed Woman'
Romance is clearly the theme – but Stevens's lady has to be the right one. He sings dismissively of fancy dancers, who move so smooth on the dance floor but have no answers, and of fine feathered friends, but all he needs is someone

117

of tougher character. Again, he starts off accompanying himself just on guitar, with strings and drums building up the sound some way in.

'Wild World'
Perhaps the album's best-known song was thought to have been inspired by and written about Stevens's previous relationship with actress Patti D'Arbanville, with whom he had lived for a while and who became the subject of his earlier single. He later explained that it was not directed specifically at her as a goodbye, but rather to any female companion, even to himself, notwithstanding the specific references addressed to a girl. It was written at a time when he was warning himself to be careful, not lose touch with home and reality, and not make the same mistakes he had as a teenage pop star at the beginning of his career. The chord sequence was modelled on one that had always been common in Spanish music. In Britain, the song was covered by Jimmy Cliff, who was played a demo by his publisher and ended up recording it, with Stevens playing some of the instruments and adding backing vocals alongside Doris Troy, as well as encouraging him to sing the high notes towards the end for added effect. Cliff's version (number eight in the UK) was not released as a single in America, leaving the field clear across the Atlantic for Stevens to reach number eleven.

'Sad Lisa'
Stevens never gave anything away about who might have inspired this song of showing deep empathy for and offering consolation to a friend, presumably suffering from depression. His piano, haunting violin and strings, and subdued vocal backing are all the additional colour this most charming of ballads needs.

'Miles From Nowhere'
Everyone goes travelling, in a spiritual sense. Life is like a mountain that he has to climb, Stevens sings, as he creeps through the valleys and gropes through the woods. It will take him to the life thereafter; his body has been a good friend, 'but I won't need it when I reach the end'. Initially accompanied by acoustic guitar and piano, just over halfway through, a softer, gentle voice takes on a deeper passion as the drums enter, speeding the whole song up for one verse and the following chorus. The drama is heightened, when after that it slows back to the original calmer pace, simply returning to guitar and piano to complete the song.

'But I Might Die Tonight'
This dwells on the insecurities of life and never knowing when one's time is up. It comes across as a gentle word of advice from the elder generation to the younger, possibly Stevens's father telling him to work hard 'and you'll find one day you'll have a job like mine'. Be straight, think right – until the final line –

'But I might die tonight'. After his close brush with death from tuberculosis, he knew what it was like to stare mortality in the face when young.

'Longer Boats'

A burst of acapella singing, bathed in echo from the backing vocalists, starts this in gospel territory, sounding like a children's song. According to Greek mythology, the souls of the departed were ferried across the river Styx to the afterlife, either heaven above or hell below. In which direction were the boats going, and which were the longest? More to the point, what allows you into heaven or sends you away? Hold on to the shore, or to your innocence, as it is the key from the door. The backing is mainly a crisp acoustic guitar, with a small touch of organ and drums towards the end.

'Into White'

The album's most delicate, poetical moment needs no more than acoustic guitar and the most tender of violin accompaniment, this goes into the magical world of verse from children's anthologies – and that is not meant in a derogatory sense – or maybe a lullaby. For interpretations of the pictures, Stevens paints in these lyrics – of building his house from barley rice, green pepper walls and water ice – one has to go online to see what others think is the message if indeed there is one. The consensus is that 'everything emptying into white' could be part of the songwriting process, transferring one's thoughts onto paper, or else a description of the dying dream before death occurs, as all images eventually empty into the colour white. Another theory suggests it is night time in the song, but dawn will bring daylight and, again, images of things seen or imagined in the dark will become white. Among those referred to in the second and third verses are 'brown-haired dogmouse', 'yellow delaney', and 'red-legged chicken', perhaps the names of flowers. An alternative theory is that Stevens wrote this song in hospital, contrasting the white all around him with the colours of the world outside. Whatever the truth or lack of it, one can hardly deny that the whole song is charm personified.

'On the Road To Find Out'

At just over five minutes, this is the album's longest song. A mid-paced number in which Stevens's voice clearly articulates his passion, he sings of leaving his happy home, his folk and friends, 'with the aim to clear my mind out'. After having 'hit the rowdy road', he is now on a spiritual quest towards personal enlightenment. This being his pre-Islam period, was it religion, the Greek Orthodox faith and Protestantism (some suggest Lutheranism) of his parents? Whichever creed, there is no misinterpreting lines like 'there's so much left to know and I'm on the road to find out', and even more pointedly, 'kick out the devil's sin, pick up a good book now' (the Bible?). The backing is mainly acoustic guitar, with a hint of backing vocals towards the end, and in the final few seconds, a few soothing notes from a church organ.

'Father and Son'

The song that went almost unnoticed at the time, but has since grown in stature, is now recognised as one of the most important, insightful songs Stevens ever wrote. It had been penned two years earlier for a musical, *Revolussia,* starring Nigel Hawthorne, about a boy who wanted to join the revolution against the wishes of his conservative father. The project never materialised due to Stevens's illness and convalescence, but he revived the song for this album. He denied the lyrics were autobiographical, saying he never really understood his own father, who, however, always let him do what he wanted instead of following him into the family business. The song, he stressed, was 'for those people who can't break loose'. The verses articulate both points of view, those of parent and youngster, and he sings them in different registers, with gentle vocal and instrumental backing from Alun Davies, as well as drums and piano.

Released as a single at the same time as the album, it failed to chart. The B-side, 'Moonshadow', appeared on Stevens's subsequent LP, *Teaser and the Firecat,* a year later, and the single was reactivated at the same time with A- and B-sides reversed, reaching the top thirty. 'Father and Son' was also recorded as a single by Sandie Shaw in 1972, by Boyzone in 1995, and as a duet by Ronan Keating (of the by-then disbanded Boyzone) and Yusuf, as Stevens was now known, in 2004, both versions getting to number two.

'Tea for the Tillerman'

The title track consists of one short verse and an even shorter chorus, the lyrics and structure of which suggest either a rather undeveloped spiritual or a kind of collage in words, taking images from the previous songs and putting them together to sound like a nursery rhyme, with the deprived children now free to play at last. Its most interesting moment comes with the ending, 'that happy day, for that happy day', with a gospel chorus joining in. Lasting precisely one minute, the feeling is that Stevens could have taken the idea further instead of leaving it as a rather perfunctory-sounding bookend to the whole record.

That does not detract from the record's well-deserved success. It immediately re-established his reputation in Britain after a short hiatus, and made him a major name in America, where he was seen as something of an English counterpart to the likes of James Taylor.

Lola Versus Powerman and the Money-Go-Round, Part One – The Kinks

Personnel:

Ray Davies: lead vocals, guitar, resonator guitar, harmonica, keyboards

Dave Davies: vocals, lead guitar, banjo

John Dalton: bass, backing vocals

Mick Avory: drums, percussion

John Gosling: keyboards

Recorded at Morgan Studios, London, April-May and August-September 1970, by Ray Davies.

UK and US release date: 27 November 1970

Record label: Pye, UK; Reprise, US

Highest chart place: Did not chart in the UK, US: 35

Running time: 40:25

All songs written by Ray Davies, unless stated otherwise.

After beginning their career with three years of almost unbroken top ten hits, The Kinks saw the 1960s out with a patchy period of diminishing chart peak positions. In 1970 they roared back with two top-five entries, destined to be their last in Britain. Both were taken from their eighth long player, for the most part, another in Ray Davies' series of concept albums, and a savage indictment of the music industry.

By this stage of their career, the group proved they could still land a well-deserved hit single, but only the really devoted fan base were still buying their albums in sufficient quantities to chart at home, greatest hits compilations aside. Yet with hindsight, this is acclaimed as among their best ten, maybe even their best five of all time. The next few 1970s concept albums divided fans and critics in their views, but few, if any, took issue with the verdict that they really excelled themselves on this one.

'The Contenders'

Forty seconds of soothing lullaby soon give way to lead guitar, boogie-woogie piano, wailing harmonica, and a rant. Davies was born to be a musician, he sings, not a mathematician, a constructor of highways or a politician, and he wants to be a winner. At once, a musical change is apparent on this album, a return to the group's early hard-rocking roots, away from the more music hall-style or wistful tone that had coloured much of their last two or three years' output. This was partly a reflection of their recent work in the concert halls in America, after a stateside ban on them had been lifted, and they realised that what audiences wanted was louder, faster, more in-your-face rock 'n' roll.

'Strangers' (Dave Davies)

The first of two songs written and sung by the younger Davies, this is one of his more reflective numbers, a folksy piece about two strangers. To a backing of acoustic guitar, piano and soothing organ, it tells of their setting out to travel the world together, maybe an analogy for musicians who meet each other early in adult life and resolve to stick together through thick and thin. Towards the end, a single organ dies away, leaving just a steady drum pattern to fade after the rest.

'Denmark Street'
Now Ray goes for the jugular. Denmark Street was at that time the central London home to the main music publishers. A jaunty singalong piano and general vaudeville-style tone do nothing to mask his bitterness as he recounts the scorn with which the suits treated him when he took his songs there in his younger days. 'I hate your music and your hair is too long,' they sneered, 'but I'll sign you up because I'd hate to be wrong.' He clearly revels in poking fun at a place where 'the walls are shaking from the tapping of feet', those of the suits unashamedly in it for the money.

'Get Back in Line'
Having damned the publishers, next it is the unions' turn. A slower song finds Ray reflecting as he stands in the dole queue, wondering whether he will go to work that day or not. In his bitterness about the power of the officials who order him not to step out of line, he is also commenting on the ban that the American Musicians' Union had placed on them for 'unprofessional behaviour' and prevented them from working there.

'Lola'
The single that put them back on the map would become one of their best-loved songs ever, reaching number two in the UK and nine in the USA. At four minutes long, one of the longest on the album, it is also musically one of the most interestingly structured with unusual chord sequences, two bridges, and the light and shade that starts it as a softly-sung number with crisp dobro or acoustic guitar one moment and an all-out rocker the next. Apart from that, there is the humour of the real-life incident that inspired it, the meeting that one of their managers had with a transvestite in a Paris nightclub. Davies recounts the confusion that resulted, even breaking into a camp accent for some lines, and the twist at the end – 'I know what I am and I'm glad I'm a man, and so is Lola'. The BBC were prepared to play the song despite any suggestiveness of sexual ambiguity, but advertising was a no-no, resulting in a last-minute re-recording of one line to change 'coca-cola' to 'cherry cola'. The former was reinstated on the album version.

'Top of the Pops'
As they say, some people only really want to know you when you're rich and famous. Cue drum roll as an announcer tells us, 'Yes, it's number one, it's *Top of the Pops*!' and they pay a back-handed tribute to the long-running

programme that almost every group or singer regarded as essential for their big break. To the sound of a bone-crunching guitar riff that recalls 'Louie Louie', Ray 'charts' the progress of their latest single – at one week, No. 11 on the BBC, No. 7 on the *NME*, *Melody Maker* wants to interview him about his political and religious views, and he has friends that he never knew he had before. For good measure, the guitar also throws in a riff from 'Land of a Thousand Dances', before the record makes it to No. 1. Now, his agent says, 'you can earn some real money'.

'The Moneygoround'
Real money? Flying pigs? Where there's a hit, there's a writ. Now we learn why our heroes don't become rich as well as famous. A swift music-hall ditty, backed largely by piano and rhythm section, and no lead break, tells all. Ray had already been through managerial and publishing disputes, leading to legal action against former managers Larry Page, Greville Collins, Robert Wace and music publisher Eddie Kassner. All but the last-named ('a foreign publisher') are mentioned by forename in the first verse, as they each take their cut from a song they have never heard, 'but they don't give a damn'. He goes to a solicitor, knowing resignedly that if he ever receives the money, he will be too old to enjoy it. Ray knew how to sound funny and deadly bitter at the same time. Before you ask, the named individuals did not apparently sue for invasion of privacy or anything else (Ray will be Ray, they probably told themselves), but they did not see the amusing side. Wace later said that neither he nor Collins ever earned anything from his songwriting. The moneygoround clearly did not stop in front of them either.

'This Time Tomorrow'
Side two starts with a brisk but wistful folk-rock number about life on the road. Musically it recalls Bob Dylan, with its bustling acoustic guitar, a touch of banjo, rolling piano and organ and a shuffling beat from the drums, while Dave Davies adds some sparing, effective vocal harmony. They leave the sun behind them, look down on fields full of houses and endless rows of crowded streets while in perpetual motion, and hardly connect with a world that does not matter much.

'A Long Way From Home'
The pace slows down on a song in which the words are addressed to an old friend (or the writer himself looking in the mirror) who has come a long way from the runny-nosed little scruff he used to be, and now thinks he is wiser because he's older, but is still a long way from home. One of the gentlest tracks, dwelling on new-found wealth and the insecurity that goes with it, this opens softly with piano, organ and acoustic guitar until the chorus moves up a gear with the rhythm section joining in. As so often, Dave Davies's backing vocal provides additional colour as the song builds in intensity.

'Rats' (Dave Davies)

Dave can always be relied on to supply two or three minutes that rock with intensity. This explodes venomously with guitar riffs, scorching organ, pulsating bass runs and drums to match, as he hits out at the people pushing him around, crazy people who have lost their heads, and a selfish man who looks at him, who was once warm and kind, but 'now all he has got is a pinstripe mind'. It lets up for a moment halfway through with a single but powerful sustained note on the guitar, but that apart delivers its message at a fair pace.

'Apeman'

In the album's other major hit, number five in the UK but 45 in the USA, half-sung and half-declaimed in a mock-Caribbean accent, Ray seeks a return to the simple life, getting away from the city, the threat of nuclear war and the crazy politicians. Again he delivers a serious message with humour and an infectious, almost calypso song (apart from a short rocking verse near the end) that defies one not to join in the chorus. Having briefly fallen foul of the BBC censors with 'Lola', he won this time round with an allusion to the air pollution a-fogging up his eyes (or something similar). It was their last British Top 10 hit, but what a triumphant way to go out on.

'Powerman'

Anger resurfaces in a chugging, hard-hitting number that pours scorn on the present-day Napoleons, Genghis Khans and others – but 'powerman don't need to fight, powerman don't need no guns'. He's got the singer's money and his publishing rights, but nothing changes – 'it's the same old story, it's the same old game'. Acoustic and electric guitars, organ and a relentless rhythm section all pile on the fury.

'Got To Be Free'

Having got all that off his chest, Ray mellows a little and reprises the opening ballad at first but then picks up speed. Musically this is brisk folk-meets-pop, with a dash of country and lively piano throughout. Ray is determined to spread the message that 'we've got to get out of this world somehow – I don't know how but I'm gonna try'.

All Things Must Pass – George Harrison

Personnel:

George Harrison: lead and backing vocals, electric and acoustic guitars, dobro, harmonica, synthesiser, harmonium

Eric Clapton: electric and acoustic guitars, backing vocals

Gary Wright: piano, organ, electric piano

Bobby Whitlock: organ, harmonium, piano, tubular bells, backing vocals

Klaus Voormann: bass, electric guitar

Ringo Starr, Jim Gordon, Ginger Baker: drums, percussion

Carl Radle: bass

Billy Preston: organ, piano

Jim Price: trumpet, trombone

Bobby Keys: saxophone

Alan White: drums, vibraphone

Pete Drake: pedal steel guitar

John Barham: harmonium, vibraphone

Pete Ham, Tom Evans, Joey Molland: acoustic guitar

Mike Gibbins: percussion

Peter Frampton: acoustic guitar

Dave Mason: electric and acoustic guitars

Tony Ashton, Gary Brooker: piano

Mal Evans: percussion

Produced at Abbey Road, Trident and Apple Studios, London, May-October 1970, by George Harrison and Phil Spector.

UK and US release date: November 1970

Highest chart places: 1 (UK), 1 (US

All songs written by George Harrison, unless stated otherwise.

All four former Beatles were productive as solo artists during 1970, none more so than George Harrison. Having stockpiled a generous catalogue of songs that always took second place to anything submitted by Lennon or McCartney for the group albums, the floodgates opened, culminating in a double album, recorded with an extensive cast of friends and colleagues, including one fellow former Beatle. Make that a triple album if you include two sides of jam sessions.

In the days when an album meant two sides of vinyl lasting anywhere between thirty and fifty minutes, on first approach, the whole album seemed a little daunting at first. On closer acquaintance, it rapidly improved. By the law of averages, there was bound to be the odd substandard moment, but at its best, the quality comes close to some of The Beatles at their finest. Fifty years later, for all its flawed moments, many people still call it the finest solo work ever released by an ex-Beatle. It set the bar high and remained something of a millstone around Harrison's neck in that he could never hope to record anything again of the same standard.

'I'd Have You Anytime' (Harrison, Dylan)

Though he did not appear on the record, the presence of Bob Dylan hovers large over two songs. Both co-wrote this sweet country-flavoured love ballad two years earlier, Harrison the verses, Dylan the bridge. Softly-strummed acoustic guitar chords, gentle organ and a crystal-clear pedal steel guitar, introduce an intricate melody built on minor and major chords. As with many of Harrison's lyrics, the meaning is ambiguous, open to interpretation in any way the listener pleases – a hymn of devotion to God or to a human partner? It is a measure of his craft as a wordsmith that one never knows.

'My Sweet Lord'

Probably the best-known two acoustic chords-intro in popular music, and the skill with which the number is gradually built up over four and a half minutes acts as a foil to the simplicity of which, stripped down to bare essentials, is little more than a chant, led by Harrison's fragile but inimitable vocal and guitar solo. The backing vocals, drums, key change upwards all come in perfectly at the right moment as the Spector wall of sound grows apace. The plagiarism case involving The Chiffons' 'He's So Fine' hardly needs repeating, although his defence that he was actually inspired by The Edwin Hawkins Singers' 'Oh Happy Day' seems fair enough. At any rate, the single topped the charts on both sides of the Atlantic in 1971, and again in Britain after Harrison's death in 2001.

'Wah-Wah'

Less a song than a groove, but what a groove, this was allegedly written by Harrison on the day he left The Beatles during the *Let It Be* sessions after a row with McCartney, and the refrain means 'you've given me a headache'. The single verse (or is it two?) says little, apart from two lines that aver 'you don't see my crying, you don't hear my sighing'. It hardly matters, for, any feelings of bitterness apart, it is a busy, exhilarating sound, based around the simplest, most infectious guitar riff and pulsating beat. Spector's wall of sound did wonders in fortifying Harrison's voice, which almost sounds too weak and unsure of itself for such a boisterous guitars, bass, keyboards and drums fest, to say nothing of the rich backing vocals. It sounded even better live as the opening track to Harrison and Friends' set on the *Concert for Bangla Desh* release in 1971, where the crowd were heard going positively delirious from the opening moments.

'Isn't It a Pity (Version 1)'

Something had to calm everything down next, and this is the first of two versions of the song that was originally favoured as the first single. There are again two short pithy verses, repeated several times, lamenting 'how we break each others' hearts, and cause each other pain'. This version lasts just over seven minutes, finishing with a lengthy fade. It was written in 1966 if not earlier, and presented during sessions for *Revolver* and *Sergeant Pepper*, then offered to Frank Sinatra. He did not record it, but others did, including Matt Monro, Dana (who both released their versions as a single in 1971), and Nina Simone.

'What Is Life'
Pared down to essentials the song is very short and simple, even slight, but the infectious combination of tune, arrangement and backing are surely a marriage made in heaven. From the opening riff to the song and that adrenalin rush of sound in the chorus, augmented towards the end by brass, this is surely the crowning glory of the full magnum opus.

'If Not For You' (Dylan)
This was introduced to the world at the same time on his album 'New Morning', but Harrison's version is superior. He treats the delicate, pleading spirit of song with more tenderness, and his harmonica work is surely the equal of that of the writer, while the organ and slide guitar match the mood perfectly.

'Behind That Locked Door'
While rumoured to be a plea to Dylan to emerge from his late 1960s seclusion, this gentle country ballad could equally be addressed to any shy or retiring partner. There is speculation that it was about his relations with John Lennon. Pedal steel guitar and shimmering organ show that Harrison had also mastered the country genre and could invest it with an emotion just as well as his peers.

'Let It Down'
Based around another of those enigmatic lyrics that could be directed to a partner or about his relationship with God, this has a bombastic intro that sounds like brass and organ, giving way to a more subdued, questioning song that really bursts into life in an oddly full-blooded chorus.

'Run of the Mill'
The heavy brass also pervades another equally questioning if not philosophical song, the final one on side two, a song title that is absent in its lyrics, and questions a relationship that seems to have gone awry: 'no one around you will love you today and throw it all away tomorrow.' One of several songs considered for inclusion on *Let It Be*, this might be Harrison addressing the other Beatles and asking where the personal and working relationships had broken down.

'Beware of Darkness'
A gentle but warning lyric and charming tune, this carries a message about avoiding the wrong people and the negative thoughts they can engender.

Although uncredited at the time, much of the guitar work was probably by Clapton.

'Apple Scruffs'

Harrison's ability to change rapidly from one mood to another in an instant shows on this folksy skiffle-style number. A fairly spontaneous tribute to the teenage fans who would hang around outside the Apple headquarters in London all day for a glimpse of one or two of their idols coming and going, with its homely acoustic guitar and harmonica, it seems that all the song is missing is a banjo or washboard. Did the Traveling Wilburys start here?

'Ballad of Sir Frankie Crisp (Let It Roll)'

Crisp was the previous owner of his home, Friar Park. Here are references to 'fools' illusions everywhere' inside the house, the 'fountain of perpetual mirth', woods and caves in the garden, all enshrined in a gentle song that borders on country territory with its steel guitar and organ sound.

'Awaiting on You All'

Cue the same bustling, big production sound of 'Wah Wah', full of backing vocals, echoing guitars, brass and multi-tracked percussion, and an overtly religious lyric – 'the Lord is awaiting on you all to awaken and see.' In praising the Lord, he also has a barbed comment (omitted from the accompanying lyrics on the inner sleeve) about the Pope who owns part of General Motors, 'the stock exchange is the only thing he's qualified to quote us'.

'All Things Must Pass'

The last song on side three, and the album's title track, is for some the most moving of all. There is speculation that he wrote it to reflect major, unhappy changes in his life, notably the illness and death of his mother and the protracted end of The Beatles. Darkness only stays at night time, he sings, but come morning, it will fade away. Times may be hard, but 'it's not always going to be this grey'. Philosophical, comforting lyrics, the stately pace and music, piano, acoustic and steel guitar have rarely been matched better on what is surely the best of the ballads here.

'I Dig Love'

A very repetitive tune, based around the title over and over again, this boasts a snappy electric piano riff, plus drums that start and stop in the right places, but in the end, fails to go anywhere on what must be the album's weakest moment.

'The Art of Dying'

The heavy philosophical message is probably best summed up in the fact that nothing in life is certain but death at the end. It drops a hint about reincarnation – 'there'll come a time when most of us return here'. If that is all too much for a three-minute song, you can put the meaning on one side and enjoy another infectious number with powerful Spector production, powerful guitar, insistent bass and drums, and the horn section giving their everything.

'Isn't It a Pity (Version 2)'
A second, shorter version than the first, with a much simpler arrangement.

'Hear Me Lord'
A slower devotional song, or rather a straightforward prayer for the forgiveness of sins in the past and help in the future. Musically, it is built mainly around a solid riff comprising brass, organ, piano and guitar, to say nothing of the backing vocals.

'Apple Jam'
Sides five and six contain five additional tracks of varying length. They were evidently fun for the musicians to record and unwind with after several hours of concentrated sessions, although some listeners may consider them self-indulgent.

'It's Johnny's Birthday' (Bill Martin, Phil Coulter, Harrison)
Basically a 90-second audio birthday card to John Lennon, based on Cliff Richard's 'Congratulations' Eurovision hit from 1968, with a touch of messing around on the vari-speed.

'Plug Me In'
Kept to a snappy three minutes, this is an energetic 12-bar blues with Harrison, Clapton and Dave Mason getting it together. Had a couple of vocal verses been added, it would have fitted comfortably within the main body of the record.

'I Remember Jeep'
Presenting almost a reconstituted Cream or Blind Faith, again with Harrison and Clapton pitting their guitars against each other on a blues boogie-based eight-minute workout, while Ginger Baker plays drums and Billy Preston adds keyboard fills.

'Thanks for the Pepperoni'
Five minutes plus of Chuck Berryish rockin' out that, once again, could have done with a couple of vocal verses.

'Out of the Blue'
Plentifully stocked with different time signatures and passages that have the horns going full blare one moment, then piano and guitar taking centre

stage, and then a touch of swirling organ, all dipping in, out and then back together for the big all-together-now finish. Although it carries on for over eleven minutes, it is far from being a formless disjointed mess but comprises several ideas that could have been worked on for three or four shorter songs or perhaps instrumentals.

Nicely Out of Tune – Lindisfarne

Personnel:
Alan Hull: vocals, acoustic 6- and 12-string guitars, keyboards
Ray Jackson: vocals, mandolin, harmonica, flatulette
Rod Clements: vocals, bass, guitars, violin, keyboards
Simon Cowe: vocals, lead and acoustic 6- and 12-string guitars, mandolin, banjo
Ray Laidlaw: drums
Produced at Trident Studios, London, August 1970, by John Anthony
UK No. 8 (1972).
UK release date: November 1970; US release date: January 1971
Record label: Charisma, UK; Elektra, US
Highest chart place: 8 UK: 8 in 1972, Did not chart in the US
Running time: 40:32
All written by Alan Hull, unless stated otherwise.

Over nearly four decades, the group who were dubbed 'the folk-rock Beatles' in their early days released fourteen studio albums. Their first, recorded from start to finish in five days, was almost unanimously acknowledged as the best they ever made, as well as a true classic of its genre. It was named thus as the group thought they were 'nicely out of tune with what everyone else was doing at the time'.

All the same, the album was presciently hailed by an enthusiastic music press on release as the debut of a group who had a bright future ahead of them. It would take the extraordinary success of their second outing, *Fog on the Tyne*, to propel them briefly into the stratosphere and send enough buyers out to put this in the charts some fourteen months after its first appearance.

'Lady Eleanor'

Always an admirer of Edgar Allan Poe's writings, Hull was said to have been inspired by two characters from his short stories, Eleanora and Roderick Usher. It is hinted in the last verse that everything as recounted in the song took place in a dream – probably the one Hull had after reading Poe one night. The climax comes after the entrance of the lady and her companion, screaming demons with tongues of fire, when a voice screams out that 'you're a liar'. Musically it makes a magnificent opening to the album, with the subdued acoustic guitar chords, gentle organ and mandolin before the first verse. Lindisfarne's trademark sweet and sour harmonies enliven the choruses, and there is a graceful coda from mandolin and bass at the end. It became their second single in the summer of 1971 and attracted some airplay, although it failed to chart until a year later when reactivated after a top-five hit from their second album (reaching number three in the UK and 83 in the US). Hull insisted that it was not 'a pop song', and was astonished that teenage fans were buying it in such huge quantities.

'Road to Kingdom Come' (Rod Clements)

Clements was an equally accomplished songwriter as well as all-around musician, although never as prolific as Hull. This was an infectious tune that would also remain a constant feature in their live set over the years. As with Clements's other songs recorded by the group at this time, Ray Jackson takes the lead vocal on a number that tells of somebody trying to work their way up in the world without much success. Yet far from being self-pitying or mournful, the result is a lively singalong given plenty of added sparkle with crisp mandolin, harmonica and lively fiddle playing.

'Winter Song'

One of the select list of numbers that initially attracted little attention outside the group's fan base, this has been acclaimed in recent times as one of the most poignant lyrics of its kind. It is not simply a seasonal tune, with its opening about how 'winter's shadowy fingers first pursue you down the street' but a Christmas song of darker hue with references to a turkey in the oven, presents having been bought, and most intriguingly of all, Santa being in his module, 'he's an American astronaut'. Hammered home at intervals is the message of how much do you really care about those less fortunate than yourself, the homeless on the street? (It pre-dated Band Aid by fourteen years in its 'thank God it's them instead of you' message). The only accompaniment to Hull's plaintive, wearily angry voice and a solo acoustic rhythm guitar is a gently rumbling bass.

'Turn a Deaf Ear' (Rab Noakes)

The first of two cover versions was written by a longtime friend of the group who sometimes supported them on tour as a solo act. While the song is pleasant enough if not really reaching the standard of most of the group's own compositions, it gives all three vocalists – Jackson, Hull and Cowe – a chance to take a verse each (two for Jackson), accompanied by a colourful mandolin riff or two and some attractive organ.

'Clear White Light (Part 2)'

There is a spiritual flavour of a kind from the opening with a marvellous harmony acapella phrase, before a steady but gentle drum pattern starts the accompaniment. What the 'clear white light' is is left to the imagination, but the feeling is that Hull is referring to a beacon of hope at the end of life's travails. The drums gather in intensity throughout the song, propelled by bass and acoustic guitar, while the chorus harmonies throughout are a delight. The last of these brings the song to a brief halt, before the drums begin again and take the song into a restrained instrumental break that fades out with a simple organ riff. It was the group's first single, and although never charting has remained a firm favourite with fans, especially on stage. 'Clear White Light (Part 1)' was neither completed nor recorded.

'We Can Swing Together'

Hull had previously recorded this as a solo single about a year before, but here he and Jackson share lead vocals. It tells of a true incident when the police were called in to break up a somewhat noisy private party one evening and were subsequently called to account for their excessively heavy-handed searching of the innocent revellers and their premises as no incriminating substances were found. Jackson's harmonica packs a punch throughout, and would do even more so when they played it live, where he would launch into a long instrumental medley of old music hall songs, jigs, reels, Geordie songs and even TV themes. Towards the end of the song, a party of all-comers join in on the chorus, making up in enthusiasm what they may lack in finesse. A wailing and rather discordant synthesiser also joins in before it fades out.

'Alan in the River With Flowers'

There is an undisguised nod towards The Beatles with this title (which does not occur in the lyrics), which apparently unsettled Elektra Records in America so much that their release renamed it 'Float Me Down the River' after the first line of the chorus. Ironically, Jackson takes lead vocal on this song about idling time away in the sunshine, although Hull joins in on the chorus, taking a leaf out of latter-day Fab Four techniques by feeding his voice through a Leslie speaker.

'Down'

Something of an oddity, not least because of the distorted intro that only plays on one channel, created by the producer to mimic the effect of an old scratched 78 r.p.m. disc. It then becomes a jaunty Hull piano-led number with something of a barbershop tone, flatulette (kazoo) in the background much of the time, and a harmonica break about halfway through. After a false ending, it returns for a few seconds with a brief reprise of the chorus, sounding a little out of tune and concentrated largely on the other stereo channel.

'The Things I Should Have Said' (Clements)

Clements's second contribution is a slow number with lyrics about a couple who find it difficult to tell each other exactly how they feel about the relationship. Some suitably restrained organ, piano and guitar work build this up towards the end.

'Jackhammer Blues' (Woody Guthrie)

On a well-timed burst of light relief, after a count-in which has been reversed on the tape, Jackson sings lead as well as contributing his usual mandolin and harmonica (accompanied on one break by handclaps) on this hoedown, while Clements's violin adds to the atmosphere. Once more it is false ending time, before they resume for the big finish with an instrumental break playing everything in unison at almost double the speed.

'Scarecrow Song'

Mostly piano- and acoustic guitar-backed, this closing ballad is addressed to a character whose lucky days are over, his Saturdays are sober and his Sundays are too long, it is not one of his best and provides a slightly anti-climactic final moment to what is the most part an extremely entertaining album that is insightful, eccentric, poignant, and downright fun in turns.

Looking On – The Move

Personnel:
Roy Wood: vocals, guitars, bass, oboe, sitar, banjo, cello, saxophones
Jeff Lynne: vocals, guitars, piano, drums, percussion
Rick Price: bass
Bev Bevan: drums, percussion
P.P. Arnold, Doris Troy: backing vocals
Produced at Advision and Philips Studios, London, May-September 1970, by Roy
Wood and Jeff Lynne.
UK release date: December 1970; US release date: January 1971
Record label: Fly, UK; Capitol, US
Did not chart in the UK or US.
Running time: 44:10
All written by Roy Wood, unless stated otherwise.

Although The Move were still releasing records, playing live dates and making
appearances on TV in 1970, they were also concentrating on the birth of the
Electric Light Orchestra. The third of their four studio albums was not only
the first completely self-penned one but also the first to feature new member
Jeff Lynne, and it is an interesting snapshot of the future directions that he
and frontman Roy Wood would take in their different groups during the
next few years. While it included two singles, much of it was dominated by
lengthy tracks that were far removed from the short snappy hits with which
they had previously been associated. Moreover, while it rocks just as hard
as Led Zeppelin, Deep Purple and others did, it also goes off at unexpected,
interesting classical tangents with the use of cello and oboe, in what could be
regarded as something of an ELO crossover, and even the odd flash of jazz.

When it was released on the new Fly label, the group had just signed a new
deal with EMI/Harvest for themselves as The Move and ELO. Fly Records were
busy promoting T. Rex who were suddenly in the ascendant, and *Looking On*
was overlooked. Bevan said he thought it 'a bit ploddy', reviews were mixed,
and it was rather overlooked. Some fans think it was their worst album ever,
others reckon it is their best. It was different, unexpected, baffling on first
listen maybe, but over the years it has become regarded as something of a
seriously underrated, even ignored heavy progressive rock masterwork that is
only now receiving its due.

'Looking On'

From the opening flourish on drums and guitar riff, the title track promises the
arrival of a new hard rock Move. One moment they sound like Black Sabbath,
the next like Cream, then Wishbone Ash. Crashing, riffing dual lead guitars
and touches of piano during the vocal section, followed by a change in time
signature with sitar and then a short drum solo, carrying proceedings into
a lengthy break that includes wah-wah guitar and even oboe until the fade.

This was the everything-but-the-kitchen-sink approach that Wood would later explore on some of the longer Wizzard album tracks a couple of years later. In one interview, he told the press that they were considering releasing it as a twelve-minute single, which would again certainly have been a first – not to say a very brave experiment.

'Turkish Tram Conductor Blues'

Basically this is a 12-bar blues with slight variations on the chord pattern. Wood sings in his now increasingly familiar growling rasp, with armour-plated guitar riffing to match. Slide guitar and – for the first time on a Move record – honking saxophone contributes to the dense sound, which comes across as slightly muddy, but effectively so. The lyrics are equally extraordinary – 'there's a rhino in the kitchen, send him on a train back home' – but then, who was really listening that hard to Move lyrics, especially with so much else going on?

On original pressings, the song was credited to Bev Bevan. Later it was revealed that the drummer had been made a gift of the credit, as a quid pro quo for his work in having done much of The Move's public relations work and press interviews while Wood and Lynne were busy with laying the foundations for ELO. Recent reissues have correctly reassigned it to Wood, though as one track on a poorly-selling album and an A-side on a German single in 1971 that flopped, any royalties would have been small.

'What?' (Jeff Lynne)

There could hardly be a greater contrast between that and the first of Lynne's songs, a stately, dreamy number on which his wistful vocal is backed largely by stately piano (do we detect a grandiose echo of a Rachmaninoff Piano Concerto in there?), gentle drums and ethereal vocal harmonies, with occasional stabs of guitar. As for the lyrics, there are questions as to 'how can they congratulate the people who destroyed the peace of mind' – perhaps an anti-war song, or perhaps just a dream, a plea for a better world. One critic called it easily the best song on what was easily The Move's least noteworthy album.

'When Alice Comes Back to the Farm'

Breathless, full tilt rock'n'roll, a thunderous feast of lead guitar riffs, fierce vocals well down in the mix, and drumming to match, and the occasional moment where all instruments cut out for a few seconds except a phrase on the cello. The saxophone is in there as well, and a couple of changes in time signature, with guitar and Lynne's boogie piano vying for honours. It was the album's second single, although it never charted.

'Open Up Said the World at the Door' (Lynne)

Another total contrast with the two songs it comes between. Strangely in view of Wood's yet-to-be-fulfilled jazz leanings, there is that kind of vibe to the first three minutes or so, even though the song is not his. Lynne's sprightly piano hovers between jazz and boogie-woogie, and he sings partly in a multi-tracked falsetto voice, while Wood fills in with short breaks firstly on sitar and then on oboe. After that, Bevan steps forward with a drum solo, part of which incorporates reversed tape, leading into a portentous, slower passage, a little reminiscent of Holst's music, with guitars, oboe and deep vocal harmonies underpinned by piano again. The effect, rather like the title track, is of two songs merged into one.

'Brontosaurus'

The album's sole hit single, reaching number seven in the UK, had revealed a very different Move to the world that summer, and not just in musical terms but also with the first appearance of Wood's out-of-this-world warpaint. A heavy deep guitar riff, a chorus about how 'she can really do the brontosaurus' which he used to say with tongue in cheek was 'a heavy rock dance number', takes up the first half, until three crisp chords on an acoustic guitar and speeded-up choruses take the song into an instrumental break dominated by Wood's slide guitar and Lynne's runs on piano.

'Feel Too Good'

Eight minutes of surprise in an album already full of surprises to those who thought they knew the group's music well. Is it soul, is it funk? Wood and Lynne were 'just messing around' in the studio after the others had gone home for the day, leaving the gear all set up, so Lynne took over the drums while Wood played bass, then added vocals and other instruments as they went along in what turned out to be a happy accident. Wood almost screams the vocal, supported ably by backing Ikettes-style singing from Doris Troy and P.P. Arnold (both uncredited on initial issues of the record) as the song is woven around riffs and outlandish solos on guitar, cello, piano and oboe before it all comes to a breathless halt, and some muffled off-mic studio laughter. Some twenty-five years later, a shortened version was included on the soundtrack to Paul Thomas Anderson's movie *Boogie Nights*.

'The Duke of Edinburgh's Lettuce' (Wood, Lynne)

The previous number segues into a hidden track – (The Move's answer to The Beatles' 'Her Majesty' on *Abbey Road*, perhaps?) For ninety seconds, Wood and Lynne gather round the piano for a charming piece of doo-wop harmony that then goes into music hall with nonsense lyrics, the piano fades, and they wish the listener goodnight.

NME TOP 30

LAST WEEK	THIS WEEK	(Week ending Wednesday, December 2, 1970)	WEEKS IN CHART	HIGHEST POSITION
3	1	I HEAR YOU KNOCKING ....Dave Edwards (NAM)	3	1
1	2	VOODOO CHILE ....Jimi Hendrix (Track)	5	1
5	3	CRACKLIN' ROSIE ....Neil Diamond (UNI)	4	3
2	4	INDIAN RESERVATION ....Don Fardon (Young Blood)	7	2
10	4	RIDE A WHITE SWAN ....T. Rex (Fly)	4	4
13	6	I'VE LOST YOU ....Elvis Presley (RCA)	3	6
26	7	HOME LOVING MAN ....Andy Williams (CBS)	2	7
6	8	WAR ....Edwin Starr (Tamla Motown)	8	2
19	9	WHEN I'M DEAD AND GONE ....McGuinness Flint (Capitol)	2	9
17	10	IT'S ONLY MAKE BELIEVE ....Glen Campbell (Capitol)	7	8
9	11	JULIE DO YA LOVE ME ....White Plains (Deram)	6	9
7	12	SAN BERNADINO ....Christie (CBS)	6	6
8	13	IT'S WONDERFUL TO BE LOVED BY YOU Jimmy Ruffin (Tamla Motown)	7	8
15	14	YOU'VE GOT ME DANGLING ON A STRING Chairmen Of The Board (Invictus)	4	14
4	15	WOODSTOCK ....Matthews Southern Comfort (UNI)	10	1
21	16	I'LL BE THERE ....Jackson Five (Tamla Motown)	3	16
16	17	WHOLE LOTTA LOVE ...........................C.C.S. (Rak)	5	13
11	18	PATCHES ....Clarence Carter (Atlantic)	9	2
28	19	MY PRAYER ....Gerry Monroe (Chapter One)	2	19
27	20	IN MY CHAIR ....Status Quo (Pye)	2	20
12	21	THE WITCH ....Rattles (Decca)	7	6
29	22	IT'S A SHAME ....Motown Spinners (Tamla Motown)	2	22
23	23	THINK ABOUT YOUR CHILDREN ....Mary Hopkin (Apple)	6	21
25	24	NEW WORLD IN THE MORNING Roger Whittaker (Columbia)	7	20
14	25	RUBY TUESDAY ....Melanie (Buddah)	8	8
●	26	NOTHING RHYMED ....Gilbert O'Sullivan (MAM)	1	26
●	27	MY WAY ....Frank Sinatra (Reprise)	15	4
17	28	ME AND MY LIFE ....Tremeloes (CBS)	11	3
22	29	BAND OF GOLD ....Freda Payne (Invictus)	13	1
●	30	LADY BARBARA ..Peter Noone and Herman's Hermits (Rak)	1	30

Above: A December chart from the NME. Spot the four names who appear in both charts in this book, rubbing shoulders with soul, rock'n'roll (Dave Edwards?), and the godfather of glam rock. `

Resources

Several books, articles and online reference sources have been consulted during research. This list is restricted to those from which direct quotes have been taken.

Books

Bilyeu, M. and others. *The Bee Gees: Tales of The Brothers Gibb* (Omnibus, 2000)

Browne, D. *Fire and Rain: The Beatles, Simon & Garfunkel, James Taylor, CSNY, and the Lost Story of 1970* (Da Capo, 2011)

Clapton, E. and Sykes, C. *Eric Clapton, The Autobiography* (Century, 2007)

Davis, S. *Hammer of the Gods: Led Zeppelin Unauthorized* (Pan, 2008)

Doggett, P. *You Never Give Me Your Money: The Battle for the Soul of The Beatles* (Bodley Head, 2009)

Fogerty, J. *Fortunate Son: My Life, My Music* (Little, Brown, 2015)

Garner, K. *The Peel Sessions* (BBC, 2007)

Harris, B. *Still Whispering After All These Years* (Michael O'Mara, 2015)

Heylin, C. *Dylan Behind the Shades* (Viking, 1991)

Napier-Bell, S. *Black Vinyl White Powder* (Random House, 2001)

Norman, P. *The Stones* (Penguin, 1993)

Reynolds, S. *Shock and Awe: Glam Rock and its Legacy* (Faber, 2016)

Rossi, F. and Parfitt, R. *Just for the Record: The Autobiography of Status Quo* (Bantam, 1993)

Sandbrook, D. *White Heat: A History of Britain in the Swinging Sixties* (Little, Brown, 2006)

Thompson, D. *Blockbuster! The True Story of The Sweet* (Cherry Red, 2010)

Townshend, P. *Who I Am* (HarperCollins, 2012)

Waksman, S. *Instruments of Desire: The Electric Guitar and the Shaping of Musical Experience* (Harvard University Press, 2001)

Articles, Reviews & Interviews

Alexander, P., 'It Broke Down Barriers: Tony Iommi On How Black Sabbath's *Paranoid* Changed The Game.' *Kerrang*, 8 October 2020

Anon. Interview with Junior Campbell. Insert notes, Marmalade, *Rainbow: The Decca Years*, Castle CD, 2000

-- Anon. Interview with Errol Brown. *Blues & Soul*, No. 1098, 2009

Dome, M. 'The Prog Interview: Keith Emerson interview. Prog online, 31 July 2015

Hilburn, R. 'Both Sides, Later.' Joni Mitchell interview. *Los Angeles Times*, 8 December 1996

Mills, M. *Very 'Eavy … Very 'Umble*, review. *Rolling Stone*, 1 October 1970

Nartez, P. *Mad Dogs and Englishmen*, review. *Rolling Stone*, 1 October 1970

Reed, R. 'How Moody Blues found new urgency with 'A Question of Balance', Justin Hayward interview. *Ultimate Classic Rock*, 7 August 2015

Robinson, P. 'Those were the days I hated', Mary Hopkin interview. *Daily Express*, 15 July 2009

Wale, M. 'Stephen Stills solo', interview. *The Times*, 12 December 1970

Wenner, J. 'Lennon Remembers, Part One.' *Rolling Stone*, 21 January 1971

Williams, R. 'Reincarnation of King Crimson.' *The Times*, 12 December 1970

On Track series

Tori Amos – Lisa Torem 978-1-78952-142-9
Asia – Peter Braidis 978-1-78952-099-6
Barclay James Harvest – Keith and Monica Domone 978-1-78952-067-5
The Beatles – Andrew Wild 978-1-78952-009-5
The Beatles Solo 1969-1980 – Andrew Wild 978-1-78952-030-9
Blue Oyster Cult – Jacob Holm-Lupo 978-1-78952-007-1
Marc Bolan and T.Rex – Peter Gallagher 978-1-78952-124-5
Kate Bush – Bill Thomas 978-1-78952-097-2
Camel – Hamish Kuzminski 978-1-78952-040-8
Caravan – Andy Boot 978-1-78952-127-6
Cardiacs – Eric Benac 978-1-78952-131-3
Eric Clapton Solo – Andrew Wild 978-1-78952-141-2
The Clash – Nick Assirati 978-1-78952-077-4
Crosby, Stills and Nash – Andrew Wild 978-1-78952-039-2
The Damned – Morgan Brown 978-1-78952-136-8
Deep Purple and Rainbow 1968-79 – Steve Pilkington 978-1-78952-002-6
Dire Straits – Andrew Wild 978-1-78952-044-6
The Doors – Tony Thompson 978-1-78952-137-5
Dream Theater – Jordan Blum 978-1-78952-050-7
Elvis Costello and The Attractions – Georg Purvis 978-1-78952-129-0
Emerson Lake and Palmer – Mike Goode 978-1-78952-000-2
Fairport Convention – Kevan Furbank 978-1-78952-051-4
Peter Gabriel – Graeme Scarfe 978-1-78952-138-2
Genesis – Stuart MacFarlane 978-1-78952-005-7
Gentle Giant – Gary Steel 978-1-78952-058-3
Gong – Kevan Furbank 978-1-78952-082-8
Hawkwind – Duncan Harris 978-1-78952-052-1
Roy Harper – Opher Goodwin 978-1-78952-130-6
Iron Maiden – Steve Pilkington 978-1-78952-061-3
Jefferson Airplane – Richard Butterworth 978-1-78952-143-6
Jethro Tull – Jordan Blum 978-1-78952-016-3
Elton John in the 1970s – Peter Kearns 978-1-78952-034-7
The Incredible String Band – Tim Moon 978-1-78952-107-8
Iron Maiden – Steve Pilkington 978-1-78952-061-3
Judas Priest – John Tucker 978-1-78952-018-7
Kansas – Kevin Cummings 978-1-78952-057-6
Led Zeppelin – Steve Pilkington 978-1-78952-151-1
Level 42 – Matt Philips 978-1-78952-102-3
Aimee Mann – Jez Rowden 978-1-78952-036-1
Joni Mitchell – Peter Kearns 978-1-78952-081-1

Also available from Sonicbond ...

The Moody Blues – Geoffrey Feakes 978-1-78952-042-2
Mike Oldfield – Ryan Yard 978-1-78952-060-6
Tom Petty – Richard James 978-1-78952-128-3
Porcupine Tree – Nick Holmes 978-1-78952-144-3
Queen – Andrew Wild 978-1-78952-003-3
Radiohead – William Allen 978-1-78952-149-8
Renaissance – David Detmer 978-1-78952-062-0
The Rolling Stones 1963-80 – Steve Pilkington 978-1-78952-017-0
The Smiths and Morrissey – Tommy Gunnarsson 978-1-78952-140-5
Steely Dan – Jez Rowden 978-1-78952-043-9
Steve Hackett – Geoffrey Feakes 978-1-78952-098-9
Thin Lizzy – Graeme Stroud 978-1-78952-064-4
Toto – Jacob Holm-Lupo 978-1-78952-019-4
U2 – Eoghan Lyng 978-1-78952-078-1
UFO – Richard James 978-1-78952-073-6
The Who – Geoffrey Feakes 978-1-78952-076-7
Roy Wood and the Move – James R Turner 978-1-78952-008-8
Van Der Graaf Generator – Dan Coffey 978-1-78952-031-6
Yes – Stephen Lambe 978-1-78952-001-9
Frank Zappa 1966 to 1979 – Eric Benac 978-1-78952-033-0
10CC – Peter Kearns 978-1-78952-054-5

Decades Series

The Bee Gees in the 1960s – Andrew Mon Hughes et al 978-1-78952-148-1
Alice Cooper in the 1970s – Chris Sutton 978-1-78952-104-7
Curved Air in the 1970s – Laura Shenton 978-1-78952-069-9
Fleetwood Mac in the 1970s – Andrew Wild 978-1-78952-105-4
Focus in the 1970s – Stephen Lambe 978-1-78952-079-8
Genesis in the 1970s – Bill Thomas 978178952-146-7
Marillion in the 1980s – Nathaniel Webb 978-1-78952-065-1
Pink Floyd In The 1970s – Georg Purvis 978-1-78952-072-9
The Sweet in the 1970s – Darren Johnson 978-1-78952-139-9
Uriah Heep in the 1970s – Steve Pilkington 978-1-78952-103-0
Yes in the 1980s – Stephen Lambe with David Watkinson 978-1-78952-125-2

On Screen series

Carry On... – Stephen Lambe 978-1-78952-004-0
David Cronenberg – Patrick Chapman 978-1-78952-071-2
Doctor Who: The David Tennant Years – Jamie Hailstone 978-1-78952-066-8
Monty Python – Steve Pilkington 978-1-78952-047-7
Seinfeld Seasons 1 to 5 – Stephen Lambe 978-1-78952-012-5

Other Books

Babysitting A Band On The Rocks – G.D. Praetorius 978-1-78952-106-1

Derek Taylor: For Your Radioactive Children – Andrew Darlington 978-1-78952-038-5

Iggy and The Stooges On Stage 1967-1974 – Per Nilsen 978-1-78952-101-6

Jon Anderson and the Warriors – the road to Yes – David Watkinson 978-1-78952-059-0

Nu Metal: A Definitive Guide – Matt Karpe 978-1-78952-063-7

Tommy Bolin: In and Out of Deep Purple – Laura Shenton 978-1-78952-070-5

Maximum Darkness – Deke Leonard 978-1-78952-048-4

Maybe I Should've Stayed In Bed – Deke Leonard 978-1-78952-053-8

Psychedelic Rock in 1967 – Kevan Furbank 978-1-78952-155-9

The Twang Dynasty – Deke Leonard 978-1-78952-049-1

and many more to come!

Would you like to write for Sonicbond Publishing?

We are mainly a music publisher, but we also occasionally publish in other genres including film and television. At Sonicbond Publishing we are always on the look-out for authors, particularly for our two main series, On Track and Decades.

Mixing fact with in depth analysis, the On Track series examines the entire recorded work of a particular musical artist or group. All genres are considered from easy listening and jazz to 60s soul to 90s pop, via rock and metal.

The Decades series singles out a particular decade in an artist or group's history and focuses on that decade in more detail than may be allowed in the On Track series.

While professional writing experience would, of course, be an advantage, the most important qualification is to have real enthusiasm and knowledge of your subject. First-time authors are welcomed, but the ability to write well in English is essential.

Sonicbond Publishing has distribution throughout Europe and North America, and all our books are also published in E-book form. Authors will be paid a royalty based on sales of their book. Further details about our books are available from www.sonicbondpublishing.com. To contact us, complete the contact form there or email info@sonicbondpublishing.co.uk